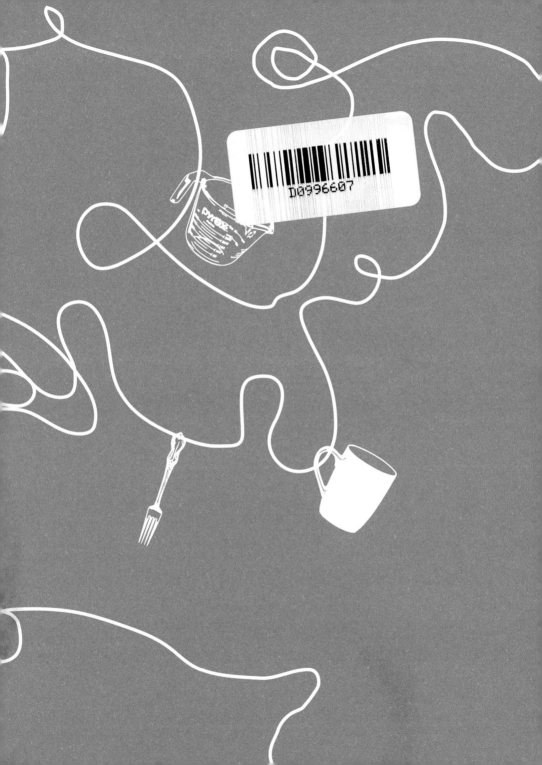

D0996607

nibbles

Published in 2012 by Hardie Grant Books

Hardie Grant Books (Australia)
Ground Floor, Building 1
658 Church Street
Richmond, Victoria 3121
www.hardiegrant.com.au

Hardie Grant Books (UK)
Dudley House, North Suite
34–35 Southampton Street
London WC2E 7HF
www.hardiegrant.co.uk

National Library of Australia Cataloguing-in-Publication data:
Nibbles: 100 sweet and savoury finger foods
ISBN 9781742704296
Appetizers. Desserts.
641.812

Publishing Director: Paul McNally
Editors: Belinda So and Hannah Koelmeyer
Design Manager: Heather Menzies
Concept Design: Lindbjerg Graphic www.lindbjerggraphic.com.au
Recipe Writers: Lee Blaylock, Michele Curtis, Kerrie Sun and Deborah Kaloper
Photographer: Marina Oliphant
Stylist: Caroline Velik
Production Manager: Penny Sanderson

Props provided by Bison Australia, ferm LIVING, Great Dane Furniture,
Mark Tuckey, Mud Australia, Nord Living and Safari Living

Colour reproduction by Splitting Image Colour Studio
Printed and bound in China by 1010 Printing International Limited

nibbles

100 sweet and savoury finger foods

hardie grant books
MELBOURNE · LONDON

contents

savoury

10 chicken meatballs wrapped in prosciutto

13 prawn and chorizo pinchos with paprika mayonnaise

14 grilled eggplant and chickpea fritters

17 salmon and mango ceviche in endive boats

18 brioche with scrambled eggs and salmon caviar

21 parmesan wafers with celeriac remoulade and roast beef

22 goat's cheese roulade on bruschetta

25 preserved lemon, chicken and radicchio quichettes

26 peking duck pancakes

29 lentil balls with lime and smoked paprika

30 ocean trout tartare with potato rösti

33 brioche with orange, fennel and grapes

34 crisp mushrooms stuffed with goat's cheese

37 caramelised onion baby tartes tatin

38 peking duck and macadamia wontons

41 wild mushroom tartlets

42 lamb filo rolls with cinnamon and currants

45 spicy onion and chickpea bhajis

46 zucchini flower fritters stuffed with feta and basil

49 prawn and ginger moneybags

50 gyoza with pork and kaffir lime

53 prosciutto, roquefort and rocket arancini

54 thai corn fritters

57 betel leaves with crab, kaffir lime and chilli

58 rabbit calzones with porcini and pine nuts

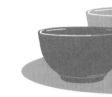

wasabi tuna with cucumber salad 61

fish and fennel pies with sourdough crust 62

crisp pork belly with chilli caramel 65

pork tostadas with chilli jam 66

manchego croquettes with sweet capsicum relish 69

crab cakes with wasabi avocado 70

cannellini bean and chorizo empanadas 73

north african tuna and preserved lemon parcels 74

pizzettes with goat's milk camembert and pickled walnut 77

smoked ham and cheddar quichettes with green tomato pickle 78

char-grilled scallops wrapped in prosciutto 81

chicken pizzettes with rosella paste and macadamia nuts 82

zucchini and haloumi fritters with roasted 85
capsicum salsa

tostadas with chipotle chicken and guacamole 86

smoked trout, lime and quail egg tartlets 89

mini duck pies with broad bean mash 90

sri lankan goat curry turnovers 93

saffron chicken pies 94

pandan chicken and black bean parcels 97

barramundi burgers with lemon myrtle mayo 98

fig galettes with jamón and pepperberry mayo 101

beef and sherry pastries 102

caramelised leek and 105
artichoke scones

cauliflower galettes with 106
taleggio and walnuts

crumpets with goat's curd 109
and lavender honey

sweet

113 raspberry cupcakes with white chocolate ganache

114 raspberry macarons with white chocolate

117 dulche de leche cupcakes

118 lemon cheesecakes with blueberry sauce

121 layered jellies with citrus and pomegranate

122 profiteroles with chocolate-espresso sauce

125 mint brownie ice-cream sandwiches

126 blood orange macarons

129 choc-mint whoopie pies with marshmallow frosting

130 vanilla cheesecake pops with ginger cookie crumbs

133 ginger whoopie pies with spiced candied-ginger cream

134 watermelon margarita pops with sweet and salty lime wedges

137 banana daiquiri cupcakes

138 s'mores cupcakes

141 lemon meringue cupcakes

142 glitter pops

145 chocolate macarons with espresso and cocoa nibs

146 brownie bites with cheesecake topping

149 gingersnap and peach ice-cream sandwiches

150 g & t pops

153 lemon madeleines with limoncello glaze

154 chocolate indulgence ice-cream sandwiches

157 pimm's pops

158 black velvet whoopie pies

161 persian rose macarons

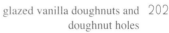

double chocolate whoopie pies 162

tangerine mimosa jellies 165

peanut macarons with salted caramel 166

passionfruit macarons 169

walnut brownie pops 170

meyer lemon bars 173

blueberry mojito popsicles 174

ice-cream cake pops 177

persian florentines 178

strawberry tartlets with sticky balsamic glaze 181

hibiscus vodka pops 182

chocolate tarts with raspberry 185

vanilla whoopee pies with white chocolate chips 186

almond corkscrews 189

black cherry and kirsch jellies 190

jelly appletinis 193

churros with chilli-chocolate sauce 194

spiced pumpkin whoopie pies with pecan mascarpone 197

pecan caramel tartlets 198

hazelnut macarons with chocolate and frangelico 201

glazed vanilla doughnuts and doughnut holes 202

warm apple pie bites 205

mini coconut cakes 206

mango lassi rum pops 209

rocky road pops 210

Savoury

makes 24

chicken meatballo
wrapped in prosciutto

500 g (1 lb 2 oz) minced
    chicken
100 g (3½ oz/1 cup) grated
    haloumi cheese
finely grated zest of
    1 lemon
2 tablespoons chopped
    flat-leaf (Italian) parsley
    or sage
1 egg yolk
50 g (1¾ oz/½ cup) dried
    breadcrumbs
sea salt and freshly
    ground black pepper
10–12 slices prosciutto

Preheat the oven to 180°C (350°F/Gas 4). Line 2 baking trays with baking paper.

Place the chicken, haloumi, lemon zest, parsley, egg yolk and breadcrumbs in a bowl, season with salt and pepper and combine well. Shape into golf-ball-sized balls.

Cut the prosciutto into thick strips, wide enough to wrap around the meatballs. Wrap each ball with a strip of prosciutto and place on the tray. Bake for 10–12 minutes until cooked through.

10

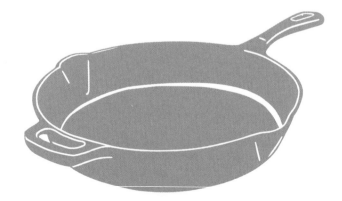

prawn and chorizo
pinchos with paprika mayonnaise

makes 24

250 g (9 oz/1 punnet)
  small cherry tomatoes,
  large ones halved
olive oil, for drizzling
sea salt
1 small baguette, cut into
  24 thin slices
1 chorizo sausage, cut into
  24 thin slices
12 cooked prawns
  (shrimp), peeled,
  deveined and halved
  lengthways
⅓ cup flat-leaf (Italian)
  parsley leaves

PAPRIKA MAYONNAISE
250 g (9 oz/1 cup)
  good-quality
  mayonnaise
1 teaspoon smoked
  sweet paprika
1 tablespoon lime juice

Preheat the oven to 180°C (350°F/Gas 4).

Place the cherry tomatoes on a baking tray, drizzle with the oil and season with salt. Roast for 10–12 minutes until just beginning to collapse.

Meanwhile, brush one side of the baguette slices with the oil, place on a baking tray and bake for 8–10 minutes until toasted and crisp.

To make the mayonnaise, combine the ingredients in a small bowl and refrigerate until required.

Preheat a barbecue or char-grill pan to high. Cook the chorizo until crisp on both sides. Drain on kitchen paper.

To serve, spread the baguette slices with the mayonnaise, top with a slice of chorizo, half a prawn, a cherry tomato and garnish with the parsley. Skewer with a toothpick to serve if desired.

13

grilled eggplant
and chickpea fritters

makes 20

1 eggplant (aubergine)
sea salt and freshly
    ground black pepper
olive oil, for cooking
225 g (8 oz/1½ cups)
    self-raising (self-
    rising) flour
250 ml (9 fl oz/1 cup) milk
2 eggs
200 g (7 oz) canned
    chickpeas (garbanzo),
    drained, rinsed and
    roughly mashed

Cut the eggplant into 1 cm (½ inch) thick slices and place on a tray. Sprinkle with salt and leave for 20 minutes or until beads of liquid form on the surface. Rinse the eggplant and dry well. Brush with a little oil and cook under a hot grill (broiler) until tender and browned on each side. Leave to cool, then roughly chop.

Place the flour in a large bowl and season with salt and pepper. Add the milk and eggs and beat until combined and smooth. Stir in the eggplant and chickpeas.

Heat a large, heavy-based frying pan over medium-high heat, add 3–4 tablespoons of oil and single tablespoon amounts of batter to the pan. Cook for 2–3 minutes on each side until golden and firm in the centre. Drain on kitchen paper and keep warm. Repeat with the remaining batter.

salmon and mango
ceviche in endive boats

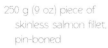

makes 24

250 g (9 oz) piece of
   skinless salmon fillet,
   pin-boned
3 tablespoons lime juice
½ teaspoon finely grated
   lime zest
½ long green chilli, finely
   diced
½ small red onion, finely
   diced
1 mango, diced
2 tablespoons chopped
   coriander (cilantro)
2 heads Belgian endive
extra-virgin olive oil,
   for drizzling
lime wedges, to serve

Cut the salmon into 5 mm (¼ inch) dice and place in a non-reactive bowl. Add the lime juice, zest, chilli and onion, and stir well. Cover and refrigerate for 20–30 minutes.

Add the mango and coriander to the ceviche and stir well.

Trim the bases of the endive, separate the leaves and arrange on a serving platter. Spoon the ceviche into the leaves and drizzle with the oil. Serve with the lime wedges.

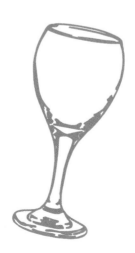

17

brioche with
scrambled eggs and salmon caviar

makes
25–30

3 eggs
2 tablespoons pouring
   (single) cream
sea salt and freshly
   ground black pepper
40 g (1½ oz) butter
50 g (1¾ oz) salmon
   caviar (roe)
snipped chives, for
   garnish

BRIOCHE DOUGH
2 x 7 g (½ oz) sachets
   dried yeast
1 teaspoon caster sugar
200 g (7 oz/1⅓ cup) plain
   (all-purpose) flour, sifted
1 teaspoon salt
2 eggs, lightly beaten
60 g (2¼ oz) unsalted
   butter, melted

To make the dough, combine the yeast, sugar and
2 tablespoons warm water in a small bowl and leave in
a warm place for 5–10 minutes until frothy.

Place the flour and salt in the bowl of an electric mixer
fitted with a dough hook, and make a well in the centre.
Add the yeast mixture, egg and butter, and mix on low
speed to combine. Knead for 6–8 minutes until smooth
and no longer sticky. Transfer to a floured bowl, cover
with a kitchen towel and leave in a warm place for
1–2 hours until doubled in size.

Preheat the oven to 190°C (375°F/Gas 5). Line 2 baking
trays with baking paper. Knock back the dough and
knead on a floured surface for 1–2 minutes. Roll pieces of
dough into 2 cm (¾ inch) balls and place on the trays.
Flatten each slightly, cover with a kitchen towel and leave
in a warm place for 20 minutes or until doubled in size.
Bake for 10–15 minutes until golden and the bottoms
sound hollow when tapped.

Whisk the eggs and cream together and season with
salt and pepper. Heat a heavy-based frying pan over
medium heat. Add the butter and egg mixture, and cook,
stirring frequently, for 3–4 minutes until just set. Remove
the pan from the heat; the residual heat in the pan will
set the eggs.

To serve, halve each brioche, fill with a spoonful of the
scrambled eggs and 4–5 pearls of salmon caviar, and
garnish with the chives.

18

parmesan wafers

with celeriac remoulade
and roast beef

makes 16

250 g (9 oz/2½ cups)
  shredded parmesan
  cheese
1 celeriac (celery root)
2 teaspoons Dijon
  mustard
2 tablespoons lemon juice
3–5 tablespoons pouring
  (single) cream
sea salt and freshly
  ground black pepper
8 slices rare roast beef,
  halved
snipped chives, for
  garnish

Preheat the oven to 180°C (350°F/Gas 4). Line 2 baking trays with baking paper. Place single tablespoon amounts of parmesan on the trays, leaving 5 cm (2 inches) between each to allow for spreading. Bake for 8–10 minutes until golden. Leave to cool on the trays.

Peel the celeriac and coarsely grate into a bowl. Add the mustard, lemon juice and enough cream to bring the mixture together. Season with salt and pepper.

To serve, top each wafer with a spoonful of the remoulade, half a slice of roast beef and garnish with the chives.

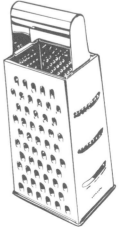

21

goat's cheese roulade
on bruschetta

1 red capsicum (pepper)
olive oil, for brushing
450 g (1 lb) eggplant, cut
    into 5 mm (¼ inch)
    thick slices
100 g (3½ oz) soft goat's
    cheese
100 g (3½ oz) cream
    cheese
½ cup basil leaves, plus
    extra for garnish
1 baguette, cut into 1.5 cm
    (⅝ inch) thick slices
extra-virgin olive oil, for
    drizzling

Preheat the oven to 180°C (350°F/Gas 4). Place the capsicum on a baking tray and roast for 20 minutes or until the skin has blackened. Transfer to a bowl, cover with plastic wrap and leave for 10 minutes. Remove the skin and seeds. Cut lengthways into 4 strips and set aside.

Preheat a barbecue or char-grill pan to medium–high. Brush both sides of the eggplant slices with olive oil and cook for 2 minutes on each side or until softened and charred. Leave to cool.

Place a large piece of aluminium foil on a surface. Arrange the eggplant, slightly overlapping so there are no gaps, in a 20 cm x 26 cm (8 inch x 10½ inch) rectangle.

Place the goat's cheese and cream cheese in a bowl and beat together until smooth. Spread onto the eggplant, scatter with the basil leaves and arrange the capsicum lengthways along the centre. Using the foil as a guide, carefully roll up along the longest side, enclosing the filling, then twist the ends to secure tightly. Refrigerate for 2 hours.

Meanwhile, lightly brush both sides of the baguette slices with olive oil. Place on baking trays and bake for 10 minutes or until lightly golden, turning once. Set aside.

To serve, cut the roulade into thin slices using a sharp knife. Place a slice on a toasted baguette slice, drizzle with the extra-virgin olive oil and garnish with basil leaves.

preserved lemon,
chicken and radicchio quichettes

makes 24

1 tablespoon olive oil
140 g (5 oz) skinless
  chicken breast fillet,
  finely diced
70 g (2⅔ oz/2 cups) finely
  chopped radicchio
¼ preserved lemon, flesh
  discarded and rind
  finely diced
freshly ground black
  pepper
2 large eggs
3 tablespoons pouring
  (single) cream
6 cherry tomatoes,
  quartered
fresh micro herbs, for
  garnish

SHORTCRUST PASTRY
300 g (10½ oz/2 cups)
  plain (all-purpose) flour
180 g (6⅓ oz) cold unsalted
  butter, cubed
pinch of salt
1 egg yolk

To make the pastry, place the flour, butter and salt in a food processor and pulse until the mixture resembles breadcrumbs. Add the egg yolk and 2 tablespoons cold water, and pulse again until just starting to come together. Knead on a floured surface to bring together, shape into a disc, wrap in plastic wrap and refrigerate for 1 hour.

Preheat the oven to 180°C (350°F/Gas 4). Lightly grease twenty-four 6 cm x 2 cm (2½ inch x ¾ inch) fluted or plain tartlet tins. Roll out the pastry to 5 mm (¼ inch) thick and, using an 8 cm (3¼ inch) round cutter, cut out 24 circles. Press each circle into the tins, trimming excess pastry. Place on baking trays and refrigerate for 30 minutes. To blind bake the cases, line them with baking paper and fill with dried beans, rice or baking weights. Bake for 15–20 minutes, remove the beans and paper and bake for a further 10–15 minutes until golden and cooked through. Remove and set aside to cool in the tins.

Meanwhile, heat the oil in a frying pan over medium-high heat. Add the chicken and cook for 1–2 minutes. Add the radicchio and preserved lemon and cook for 2 minutes or until the chicken is cooked through and the radicchio is wilted. Season with pepper.

Divide the mixture between the cases. Whisk the eggs and cream together in a jug and pour into the cases. Bake for 15–20 minutes until golden and set. Cool slightly and remove from tins.

To serve, top each quichette with a tomato quarter and garnish with the herbs.

peking duck
pancakes

200 g (7 oz) pre-cooked
    duck breast, skin
    discarded
hoisin sauce, for
    spreading and dipping
¼ iceberg lettuce,
    shredded
1 Lebanese (short)
    cucumber, cut into
    long, thin strips
1 cup coriander (cilantro)
    leaves

PANCAKES
1 egg
250 ml (9 fl oz/1 cup) milk
pinch of salt
150 g (5½ oz/1 cup) plain
    (all-purpose) flour
1 tablespoon snipped
    chives
30 g (1 oz) butter, melted

To make the pancake batter, lightly whisk the egg, milk and salt together in a bowl. Whisk in the flour, a little at a time, until the batter is the consistency of thin custard. Leave to rest for 30 minutes. Strain the batter, if there are any lumps. Stir through the chives.

Heat a small, heavy-based frying pan over medium heat. Brush the pan with the butter and pour in just enough batter to form a 10 cm (4 inch) pancake. Cook for 1–2 minutes until golden, then flip over and cook the other side until golden. Remove from the pan and repeat with the remaining batter.

Preheat the oven to 180°C (350°F/Gas 4). Place the duck on a baking tray and bake for 8–10 minutes until just heated through. Remove and thinly slice.

To serve, gently warm the pancakes in the oven. Lay the pancakes on a surface and spread with a little hoisin sauce. Place 1–2 slices of duck, some lettuce, cucumber and coriander leaves in the centre of each pancake and roll up. Serve with extra hoisin sauce for dipping.

lentil balls with
lime and smoked paprika

makes 30

2 tablespoons olive oil
1 onion, finely diced
1 carrot, finely diced
1 teaspoon smoked
    sweet paprika
1 teaspoon harissa
180 g (1 cup) red lentils,
    rinsed
500 ml (18 fl oz/2 cups)
    vegetable stock
½ cup chopped coriander
    (cilantro)
finely grated zest of
    2 limes
1 egg
50–100 g (1¾–3½ oz/
    ½–1 cup) dried
    breadcrumbs
sea salt and freshly
    ground black pepper
vegetable oil, for
    deep-frying

Heat the olive oil in a saucepan over medium heat, add the onion and carrot, and sauté for 3–4 minutes until softened or translucent. Stir in the paprika and harissa and cook for 30 seconds. Add the lentils and stir well. Pour in enough stock to cover, bring to the boil, reduce the heat and simmer, adding more stock as necessary, for 15 minutes or until the lentils are tender and all the liquid has been absorbed. Transfer to a bowl and leave to cool slightly.

Add the coriander, lime zest and egg to the lentil mixture along with enough breadcrumbs to bring the mix just together but is not too dry. Season with salt and pepper. Roll the mixture into golf-ball-sized balls.

Heat the vegetable oil in a deep-fryer or large, heavy-based saucepan to 180°C (350°F) and deep-fry 6–8 balls at a time for 3–4 minutes until golden. Drain on kitchen paper. Sprinkle with salt and serve.

29

ocean trout tartare
with potato rösti

500 g (1 lb 2 oz) potatoes
4 spring onions (scallions),
   thinly sliced
sea salt and freshly
   ground black pepper
vegetable oil, for
   shallow-frying
250 g (9 oz) piece of
   skinless ocean trout
   fillet, pin-boned
2 tablespoons lime juice
wasabi paste, for
   spreading
2 tablespoons pickled
   ginger, finely diced
snipped chives, for
   garnish

Peel and finely grate the potatoes. Wrap in a kitchen towel and wring out to remove excess moisture. Transfer to a small bowl, combine with the spring onion and season with salt and pepper. Roll 2-tablespoon amounts of mixture into tight balls, then flatten into patties.

Heat 5 mm (¼ inch) oil in a large, heavy-based frying pan over medium heat, add the rösti mixture, in batches, and cook until golden on both sides. Remove, drain on kitchen paper and keep warm.

Finely dice the ocean trout, combine with the lime juice and season.

To serve, spread a little wasabi over each rösti, top with 1 heaped teaspoon of trout tartare and garnish with the pickled ginger and chives.

brioche with orange,
fennel and grapes

makes 24

3 tablespoons milk

2 tablespoons caster (superfine) sugar

1 x 7 g (¼ oz) sachet dried yeast

300 g (10½ oz/2 cups) plain (all-purpose) flour, sifted, plus extra for dusting

finely grated zest of 1 orange

1 tablespoon fennel seeds, toasted and ground

3 eggs, lightly beaten

120 g (4¼ oz) unsalted butter, cubed and at room temperature

2 egg yolks, lightly beaten

250 g (9 oz) soft goat's cheese

24 grapes, halved lengthways

Combine the milk, sugar and yeast in a small bowl, set aside in a warm place for 5–10 minutes until frothy and the sugar has dissolved.

Place the flour, orange zest and ground fennel in the bowl of an electric mixer fitted with a dough hook and make a well in the centre. Add the egg and the yeast mixture and mix on low speed to combine. Mix in the butter, in batches, until well incorporated. Continue mixing for 10–15 minutes until the dough is soft, glossy and comes away from the side of the bowl. Transfer to a floured bowl, cover with a kitchen towel and leave in a warm place for 1½ hours or until doubled in size.

Preheat the oven to 180°C (350°F/Gas 4). Lightly grease twenty-four 6 cm x 2 cm (2½ inch x ¾ inch) fluted brioche moulds. Knock back the dough and divide into 24 pieces. Shape each into a ball and place in the moulds. Cover with a kitchen towel and leave in a warm place for 30 minutes or until doubled in size. Brush the tops with the egg yolk and bake for 25 minutes or until golden and the bottoms sound hollow when tapped. Turn out from the moulds and cool on a wire rack.

To serve, make a 3 cm (1¼ inch) long incision along the top of the brioche on an angle to reach halfway down and fill the pocket with the goat's cheese and grape halves.

33

crisp mushrooms
stuffed with goat's cheese

150 g (5½ oz) soft goat's
  cheese or ricotta
2 garlic cloves, crushed
2 tablespoons chopped
  mixed herbs, such as
  basil, parsley, thyme
  or oregano
1 tablespoon thickened
  cream
freshly ground black
  pepper
24 button mushrooms
1 egg
125 ml (4½ fl oz/½ cup)
  milk
plain (all-purpose) flour,
  for coating
100 g (3½ oz/1 cup)
  dried breadcrumbs
vegetable oil, for
  deep-frying

Combine the goat's cheese, garlic, herbs and cream
in a bowl and season with pepper. Remove the stems
from the mushrooms. Use a teaspoon to spoon the
mixture into the mushroom caps, rounding the tops
to form 'balls'.

Lightly whisk the egg and milk together in a bowl.
Place the flour and breadcrumbs in separate shallow
dishes. Working with one mushroom at a time, coat lightly
in flour, then dip in the eggwash and coat in
the breadcrumbs. Repeat so that the mushrooms are
double coated to prevent any leakage during cooking.

Heat the oil in a deep-fryer or large, heavy-based
saucepan to 180°C (350°F) and deep-fry 6–8 mushrooms
at a time for 3–4 minutes until golden. Drain on
kitchen paper.

34

caramelised onion
baby tartes tatin

makes 20

80 ml (2½ fl oz/⅓ cup)
   olive oil
3 onions, thinly sliced
2 sprigs thyme
sea salt and freshly
   ground black pepper
50 g (1¾ oz/½ cup)
   grated cheddar cheese

DOUGH
250 g (9 oz/1⅔ cups)
   self-raising (self-rising)
   flour
1 teaspoon salt
100 ml (3½ fl oz) milk
40 g (1½ oz) butter, melted
1 teaspoon Dijon mustard
1 egg

Place the oil, onion and thyme in a frying pan over low heat and cook, stirring regularly, for 20–30 minutes until softened and caramelised. Season with salt and pepper.

Preheat the oven to 180°C (350°F/Gas 4). Lightly grease two 12-hole mini-muffin trays.

Meanwhile, to make the dough, sift the flour and salt into a bowl and make a well in the centre. Whisk the milk, butter, mustard and egg together in a separate bowl. Add to the dry ingredients and mix with a fork until the dough just comes together. Knead briefly on a floured surface until smooth. Roll out to 1 cm (½ inch) thick and, using a 2.5 cm (1 inch) round cutter, cut into 20 circles.

Place a spoonful of onion in the base of each mini-muffin hole, sprinkle with some cheese and top with a circle of dough. Bake for 10–15 minutes until golden. Leave in tins for 3–4 minutes. To remove the tartes, cover each tray with a large plate and invert the tartes onto the plate.

37

peking duck
and macadamia wontons

200 g (7 oz) pre-cooked
duck breast, skin
discarded
2 tablespoons grated
ginger
2 spring onions (scallions),
chopped
2 tablespoons chopped
coriander (cilantro)
40 g (1½ oz/¼ cup)
macadamia nuts,
chopped
1 tablespoon hoisin sauce
2 teaspoons soy sauce
1 x 250 g (9 oz) packet
wonton wrappers

CHILLI-SOY DIPPING
SAUCE
80 ml (2½ fl oz/⅓ cup)
soy sauce
2 small red chillies,
chopped

To make the dipping sauce, combine the ingredients
in a small bowl and set aside.

Finely dice the duck meat and combine with the
ginger, spring onion, coriander, macadamia nuts, hoisin
sauce and soy sauce.

Lay 6–8 wonton wrappers on a surface. Keep the rest
of the wrappers covered with a damp kitchen towel to
prevent them from drying out. Place 1 teaspoon of duck
mixture in the centre of each wrapper. Brush 2 edges with
water, fold each wonton in half and press edges together
firmly to seal. Repeat with remaining wrappers and
mixture.

Bring a saucepan of water to the boil. Add wontons,
in batches of 6–8, and poach for 3–4 minutes until the
wrapper is translucent.

Serve with the dipping sauce.

Note: Rather than folding the wontons, make
a circle with your thumb and index finger and
gently push the dumpling down through the
circle to make a barrel shape. Place
the wontons into a bamboo steamer
and steam over boiling water, in
batches, for 10–15 minutes.

wild mushroom
tartlets

makes 30–35

10 g (⅓ oz) dried porcini
   mushrooms
2 tablespoons olive oil
1 onion, finely diced
250 g (9 oz) wild
   mushrooms, sliced
2 garlic cloves, crushed
80 ml (2½ fl oz/⅓ cup)
   white wine
2 tablespoons chopped
   flat-leaf (Italian) parsley
   or basil
sea salt and freshly
   ground black pepper
35 savoury tartlet shells
fresh flat-leaf (Italian)
   parsley leaves, for
   garnish

Pour 250 ml (9 fl oz/1 cup) boiling water over the porcini mushrooms and leave for 20 minutes. Drain, reserving the porcini and soaking liquid.

Heat the oil in a saucepan over medium–high heat, add the onion and cook for 3–4 minutes until softened and translucent. Add the wild mushrooms and cook, stirring often, for 4–5 minutes until softened. Add the garlic and porcini and cook for 1–2 minutes until fragrant. Add the wine and cook until the liquid has reduced by half. Add the reserved porcini liquid and bring to the boil. Reduce the heat and simmer for 10–15 minutes until all the liquid has evaporated. Add the chopped parsley and season with salt and pepper.

Spoon the hot mushroom mixture into the tartlet shells. Garnish with the parsley leaves.

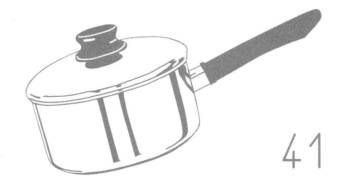

41

lamb filo rollo
with cinnamon and currants

2 tablespoons olive oil
3 French shallots,
    finely chopped
3 garlic cloves, crushed
½ teaspoon ground
    ginger
1 teaspoon ground
    cinnamon
¼ teaspoon ground
    cloves
400 g (14 oz) minced lamb
250 g (9 oz/1 cup) canned
    diced tomato
1 tablespoon tomato paste
    (concentrated purée)
250 ml (9 fl oz/1 cup)
    chicken stock
50 g (1¾ oz/⅓ cup)
    currants
2 tablespoons chopped
    almonds
sea salt and freshly
    ground black pepper
375 g (13 oz) filo pastry
melted butter, for
    brushing
ground cinnamon,
    to serve

Preheat the oven to 180°C (350°F/Gas 4). Line 2 baking trays with baking paper.

Heat the oil in a saucepan over medium–high heat, add the shallots and garlic and sauté for 2–3 minutes until softened and translucent. Add the ginger, cinnamon, cloves and lamb, and cook, breaking up any lumps with a wooden spoon, for 5 minutes or until browned. Add the tomato, tomato paste and stock, then cover and simmer for 10 minutes. Remove the lid and cook for a further 10 minutes or until the liquid has almost evaporated. Stir the currants and almonds through and season with salt and pepper.

Lay a sheet of filo on a surface with the short end closest to you, brush generously with the butter and top with another sheet of filo. Repeat once more. Keep the rest of the filo covered with a damp kitchen towel to prevent it from drying out. Cut the buttered filo lengthways into thirds. Place 1 tablespoon of mixture on each of the short ends, fold in the sides to encase the filling and roll each up into a cigar. Seal the ends, place on the trays and brush the tops with butter. Repeat with the remaining filo and mixture. Bake for 15–25 minutes until golden.

To serve, sprinkle with the cinnamon.

spicy onion
and chickpea bhajis

3 onions, finely diced
150 g (5½ oz/1 cup) chickpea (besan) flour
150 g (5½ oz/1 cup) plain (all-purpose) flour
2 teaspoons baking powder
3 teaspoons ground cumin
3 teaspoons ground coriander
1 teaspoon sea salt
1 egg
400 g (14 oz) canned chickpeas (garbanzo), drained, rinsed and roughly mashed
⅓ cup chopped coriander (cilantro)
vegetable oil, for shallow-frying
Greek-style yoghurt, to serve

Blanch the onions in a saucepan of boiling water. Drain, reserving the onion and 250 ml (9 fl oz/1 cup) cooking liquid.

Place the chickpea flour, plain flour, baking powder, ground cumin and coriander, and salt in a bowl and make a well in the centre. Add the egg and reserved cooking liquid and whisk together until smooth. Add the onion, chickpeas and chopped coriander, and mix well.

Heat 4 cm (1½ inches) oil in a large, heavy-based saucepan or wok over medium–high heat. Add single tablespoon amounts of mixture to the pan and cook until golden on both sides. Drain on kitchen paper and keep warm. Repeat with the remaining mixture.

Serve with yoghurt for dipping.

zucchini flower
fritters stuffed with feta and basil

makes 16

150 g (5½ oz/1 cup) plain
   (all-purpose) flour
sea salt and freshly
   ground black pepper
1 egg, separated
1 teaspoon olive oil
16 zucchini flowers
   (squash blossoms)
150 g (5½ oz) soft
   (Persian) feta
10 basil leaves, chopped
vegetable oil, for
   shallow-frying

Sift the flour and ½ teaspoon salt together in a bowl and make a well in the centre. Whisk the egg yolk, olive oil and 250 ml (9 fl oz/1 cup) water together in a bowl. Add to the flour and whisk until combined. Leave batter to rest for 30 minutes.

Meanwhile, gently open each zucchini flower and remove the stamen. Wash gently, if needed, and dry well. Roughly mash the feta using a fork. Add the basil and season with pepper. Place 1 heaped teaspoon of filling into each flower and firmly press the petals around the filling to enclose.

Heat 5 cm (2 inches) vegetable oil in a large, heavy-based saucepan or wok over medium–high heat.

Beat the egg white until soft peaks form, then fold through the batter. Dip the zucchini flowers into the batter one at a time, then place in the hot oil and cook for 4–5 minutes until golden. Drain on kitchen paper and season with salt.

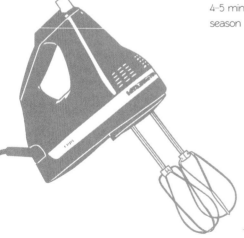

prawn and ginger
money bags

makes 30

200 g (7 oz) minced
   prawn (shrimp)
1 garlic clove, crushed
4 spring onions (scallions),
   thinly sliced
2 teaspoons grated
   ginger
1 tablespoon chopped
   coriander (cilantro)
1 tablespoon soy sauce
1 x 250 g (9 oz) packet
   gyoza wrappers
fresh chives, to tie around
   money bags
vegetable oil, for
   deep-frying
sweet chilli sauce,
   for dipping

Combine the prawn, garlic, spring onion, ginger, coriander and soy sauce in a bowl.

Lay 6–8 gyoza wrappers on a surface. Keep the rest of the wrappers covered with a damp kitchen towel to prevent them from drying out. Place 1 teaspoon of prawn mixture in the centre of each wrapper. Brush the edge with water, fold up the sides around the filling to form a pouch, pinch at the top to enclose and tie up with a chive to secure. Repeat with the remaining wrappers and mixture.

Heat the oil in a deep-fryer or large, heavy-based saucepan to 180°C (350°F) and deep-fry the money bags, in batches, turning occasionally, for 3–4 minutes until golden and cooked through. Drain on kitchen paper and keep warm. Serve with the sweet chilli sauce.

gyoza with pork
and kaffir lime

makes 50

400 g (14 oz) lean minced pork

50 g (1¾ oz/1 cup) finely shredded Chinese cabbage (wombok)

4 spring onions (scallions), sliced

1 teaspoon sesame oil

1 tablespoon soy sauce, plus extra for drizzling

2 teaspoons grated ginger

2 garlic cloves, crushed

2 kaffir lime leaves, finely chopped

1 x 200 g (7 oz) packet gyoza wrappers

peanut oil, for cooking

Combine the pork, cabbage, spring onion, sesame oil, soy sauce, ginger, garlic and lime leaves in a bowl.

Lay 6–8 wrappers on a surface. Keep the rest of the wrappers covered with a damp kitchen towel to prevent them from drying out. Place 1 teaspoon of pork mixture in the centre of each wrapper. Brush the edge with water, fold in half, pressing the edge together to seal. Repeat with the remaining wrappers and mixture.

Heat a large, heavy-based frying pan over medium–high heat, add 2 tablespoons oil and 10–12 dumplings but do not overcrowd. Cook for 2–3 minutes until crisp on one side, then add 125 ml (4½ fl oz/½ cup) boiling water, cover, reduce the heat and simmer for 5–6 minutes until gyoza are cooked through. Remove from the heat, add a splash of soy to the pan and serve gyoza with pan juices. Repeat with the remaining gyoza.

prosciutto, roquefort
and rocket arancini

makes 30

6 slices prosciutto
2 tablespoons olive oil
1 onion, finely diced
1 garlic clove, crushed
1 leek, white part only, thinly
    sliced (optional)
1 carrot, finely diced
    (optional)
200 g (7 oz/1 cup) arborio
    rice
125 ml (4½ fl oz/½ cup)
    white wine
750 ml–1 litre (26–36 fl oz/
    3–4 cups) hot vegetable
    or chicken stock
50 g (1¾ oz/½ cup) grated
    parmesan cheese
100 g (3½ oz) Roquefort or
    other blue cheese
50 g (1¾ oz) rocket
    (arugula) leaves, chopped
2 tablespoons chopped
    flat-leaf (Italian) parsley
sea salt and freshly ground
    black pepper
1 egg
125 ml (4½ fl oz/½ cup) milk
120 g (4¼ oz/2 cups) panko
    (Japanese) breadcrumbs
vegetable oil, for deep-
    frying

Heat a heavy-based frying pan over medium–high heat, add the prosciutto and cook for 2–3 minutes on each side until crisp. Chop and set aside.

Heat a large, heavy-based saucepan over medium heat, add the olive oil, onion and garlic, and leek and carrot, if using, and sauté for 3–4 minutes until the vegetables have softened and the onion and leek are translucent. Add the rice, stir to coat in the oil, and cook for 1 minute. Add the wine and stir until absorbed.

Add enough stock to just cover the rice, and stir until absorbed. Continue adding stock a ladleful at a time as each addition is absorbed, stirring well after each ladleful. After 15–20 minutes the rice should be nearly cooked; each grain should still be slightly firm in the centre. Remove from the heat. Add the prosciutto, cheeses, rocket and parsley and stir until the cheese has melted and the risotto is creamy. Season with pepper.

When the risotto is cool enough to handle, roll the mixture into golf-ball-sized balls. Lightly whisk the egg and milk together. Place the breadcrumbs in a shallow bowl. Working with one ball at a time, dip each ball in the eggwash, then coat in the breadcrumbs.

Heat the vegetable oil in a deep-fryer or large, heavy-based saucepan to 180°C (350°F) and deep-fry 6–8 balls at a time for 3–4 minutes until golden. Drain on kitchen paper. Sprinkle with salt to serve.

53

thai corn fritters

makes 30

150 g (5½ oz/1 cup)
self-raising
(self-rising) flour, plus
1–2 tablespoons extra
180 g (6½ oz/1¼ cups)
polenta
½ teaspoon baking
powder
½ teaspoon salt
1 egg
250 ml (9 fl oz/1 cup) milk,
plus 1–2 tablespoons
extra
400 g (14 oz/2 cups)
canned corn kernels,
drained
½ cup chopped coriander
(cilantro)
4 spring onions (scallions),
thinly sliced
1 small red chilli, seeds
removed and diced
vegetable oil, for
shallow-frying
fresh coriander leaves,
for garnish
sweet chilli sauce,
for dipping

Combine the flour, polenta, baking powder and salt in a bowl and make a well in the centre. Add the egg and milk, and mix until smooth. Add the corn, chopped coriander, spring onion and chilli, and stir well. If the mixture seems too thin, add 1–2 tablespoons extra flour; if it is too thick, add 1–2 tablespoons extra milk.

Heat a large, heavy-based frying pan over medium heat, add 1–2 tablespoons oil and single tablespoon amounts of mixture and cook for 2–3 minutes until crisp and bubbles have formed on the top, then flip over and cook the other side until golden. Remove from the pan and keep warm. Repeat with the remaining mixture. Garnish with the coriander leaves and serve with the sweet chilli sauce.

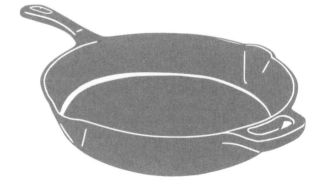

betel leaves
with crab, kaffir lime and chilli

makes 20

150 g (5½ oz) cooked
   crabmeat
1 long red chilli, seeds
   removed and sliced
2 kaffir lime leaves, thinly
   sliced
1 cup coriander (cilantro)
   leaves
1 red (Asian) shallot, diced
4 mint leaves, thinly sliced
1 tablespoon fried shallots
1 tablespoon lime juice
1 tablespoon fish sauce
20 betel leaves (see note)
50 g (1¾ oz) salmon
   caviar (roe) (optional)

Combine all of the ingredients, except the betel leaves and salmon caviar, in a large bowl. Lay the betel leaves flat on a surface. Divide the mixture between the leaves and top with a few pearls of salmon caviar, if using.

Note: Betel leaves are available from Thai grocers.

57

rabbit calzones
with porcini and pine nuts

makes 20

15 g (½ oz) dried porcini
   mushrooms, soaked
   in 125 ml (4½ fl oz/
   ½ cup) hot water for
   20 minutes
3 tablespoons olive oil
600 g (1 lb 5 oz/about ½)
   farmed rabbit, cut into
   pieces
3 French shallots, finely
   diced
2 garlic cloves, crushed
4 sprigs thyme
1 small carrot, finely diced
125 ml (4½ fl oz/½ cup)
   white wine
125 ml (4½ fl oz/½ cup)
   chicken stock
1 x quantity pizza dough
   (see page 77)
1½ tablespoons tomato
   paste (concentrated
   purée)
40 g (1½ oz/¼ cup) pine
   nuts, toasted and
   chopped
50 g (1¾ oz/½ cup) finely
   grated parmesan
   cheese

Preheat the oven to 180°C (350°F/Gas 4).

Drain the mushrooms, reserving the liquid, and finely dice. Heat 2 tablespoons of oil in a large, heavy-based, ovenproof saucepan over medium–high heat. Add the rabbit and brown all over. Remove from the pan and set aside. Add the remaining oil and the shallots, garlic and thyme to the pan and sauté for 2–3 minutes until softened and translucent. Add the carrot and cook for 2 minutes. Add the mushrooms, wine, stock and the reserved porcini liquid. Bring to the boil, cover, transfer to the oven and bake for 1½ hours or until the meat is falling off the bones.

Meanwhile, make the pizza dough (see page 77) and leave in a warm place for 1 hour.

Remove the rabbit from the pan and shred the meat from the bones. Place the pan back over medium–low heat, add the tomato paste and cook for 10–15 minutes until the sauce has thickened. Add the rabbit and pine nuts and stir through. Cool.

Preheat the oven to 220°C (425°F/Gas 7). Lightly oil 2 baking trays. Knock back the dough and divide into 20 pieces. Roll each into a ball, place on a floured surface, cover with a kitchen towel and leave for 20–30 minutes until doubled in size. Flatten each ball into an 8 cm (3¼ inch) round. Place 1 tablespoon of filling onto one half of each round and sprinkle with parmesan. Fold in half and twist the edges together to seal. Place on the trays, brush with oil and bake for 10–15 minutes until golden.

wasabi tuna
with cucumber salad

Makes 25–30

1 tablespoon dried
  wakame (see note)
1 Lebanese (short)
  cucumber, seeds
  removed and
  thinly sliced
2 tablespoons pickled
  ginger, thinly sliced
1 tablespoon black
  sesame seeds
1 x 450–500 g
  (1 lb–1 lb 2 oz) piece
  of yellowfin tuna
3 tablespoons
  vegetable oil
soy sauce, for drizzling

SPICE MIX
1 tablespoon cumin seeds
2 tablespoons coriander
  seeds
1 tablespoon almonds
2 tablespoons wasabi
  powder

To make the spice mix, heat a frying pan over medium–high heat. Add the cumin and coriander seeds and toast until the seeds are fragrant and have started to pop. Leave to cool. Place the almonds in a spice grinder and grind to fine crumbs. Transfer to a bowl. Place the toasted seeds in the spice grinder and coarsely grind. Add to the ground almonds along with the wasabi powder, and mix well. Place on a plate and set aside.

Soak the wakame in a bowl of water for 5 minutes or until softened. Drain well. Roughly chop and combine with the cucumber, pickled ginger and sesame seeds.

Cut the tuna into 10 cm (4 inch) long pieces and coat well in the spice mix.

Heat the oil in a heavy-based frying pan over high heat, add the tuna and cook for 1 minute on each side or until seared but still pink in the middle; be careful not to overcook. Transfer to a chopping board and, using a sharp knife, cut each piece into five 2 cm (¾ inch) thick pieces.

To serve, place 1 heaped teaspoon of cucumber salad in a small bowl, top with a piece of tuna and drizzle with a little soy sauce.

Note: Dried wakame, a type of seaweed, is available from Asian grocers.

61

fish and fennel
pies with sourdough crust

1 x quantity shortcrust
   pastry (see page 89)
50 g (1¾ oz) butter
1 small onion, finely diced
1 baby fennel, thinly sliced
40 g (1½ oz) plain
   (all-purpose) flour
375 ml (13 fl oz/1½ cups)
   hot fish stock
350 g (12 oz) skinless firm
   white fish fillets, cut
   into small cubes
3 tablespoons pouring
   (single) cream
¼ cup chopped flat-leaf
   (Italian) parsley
sea salt and freshly
   ground black pepper
2–3 slices day-old
   sourdough, crusts
   removed
25 g (1 oz/¼ cup) finely
   grated parmesan
   cheese
¼ cup dill leaves
mayonnaise, to serve
lemon wedges, to serve

Make the shortcrust pastry dough (see page 89) and refrigerate for 1 hour.

Meanwhile, heat the butter in a large, heavy-based saucepan over medium–high heat, add the onion and fennel and sauté for 2–3 minutes until softened and translucent. Add the flour and mix well. Add 125 ml (4½ fl oz/½ cup) of stock and stir well, ensuring there are no lumps. Gradually add the remaining stock, stirring well. Add the fish, reduce the heat and simmer for 10 minutes, stirring gently until the sauce has thickened. Stir the cream and parsley through, and season with salt and pepper. Leave to cool.

Process the bread in a food processor until roughly chopped. Transfer to a bowl and stir through the parmesan and dill.

Preheat the oven to 190°C (375°F/Gas 5). Lightly grease twenty 6 cm x 2.5 cm (2½ inch x 1 inch) pie tins. Roll out the pastry to 5 mm (¼ inch) thick and, using an 8 cm (3¼ inch) round cutter, cut out 20 circles. Press each circle into the tins, trimming excess pastry. Divide the fish mixture between the tins, top with the breadcrumb mixture and bake for 20–25 minutes until the tops are golden. Leave to cool slightly, then remove from the tins using a butter knife.

Serve with the mayonnaise and lemon wedges.

250 g (9 oz) caster
  (superfine) sugar
200 ml (7 fl oz) fish sauce
3 tablespoons light
  soy sauce
2 small red chillies,
  finely chopped
3 star anise

crisp pork belly
with chilli caramel

1 stalk lemongrass,
   bruised and chopped
4 garlic cloves, chopped
4 red (Asian) shallots,
   chopped
40 g (1½ oz) ginger,
   chopped
2 long red chillies,
   chopped,
finely grated zest of 1 lime
1 bunch coriander
   (cilantro), plus roots,
   chopped (reserve a
   few leaves for garnish)
vegetable oil, for cooking
125 ml (4½ fl oz/½ cup)
   soy sauce
2 tablespoons fish sauce
2 tablespoons grated
   palm sugar
1 kg (2 lb 4 oz) piece
   of pork belly,
   rind removed
tapioca flour, rice flour or
   cornflour, for dusting

Preheat the oven to 170°C (325°F/Gas 3).

Place the lemongrass, garlic, shallots, ginger, chilli, lime zest and coriander in a food processor. Process to a coarse paste.

Heat 2 tablespoons of oil in a large, heavy-based, ovenproof saucepan over medium-high heat, add the paste and sauté for 2 minutes or until fragrant. Add the soy sauce, fish sauce, palm sugar and 375 ml (13 fl oz/1½ cups) water, and bring to the boil. Add the pork, cover and bake for 1½ hours or until the pork is tender when pierced with a knife. Leave to cool for 4–5 hours.

To make the chilli caramel, dissolve the sugar in 250 ml (9 fl oz/1 cup) water in a saucepan over medium-low heat. Gently bring to the boil, reduce the heat and simmer for 15 minutes or until light golden. Do not stir but occasionally brush down the sides of the pan with water to prevent the sugar from crystallising. Remove from the heat and add 2 tablespoons of water; be very careful as the caramel may spit. Stir in the fish sauce, soy sauce, chilli and star anise. Leave for 1 hour to infuse.

Heat the oil in a deep-fryer or large, heavy-based saucepan to 180°C (350°F). Cut the pork into 2 cm (¾ inch) cubes, dust in the flour and deep-fry for 3–4 minutes until golden. Drain on kitchen paper.

To serve, divide the pork into small bowls, drizzle with the chilli caramel and garnish with the reserved coriander leaves.

pork tostadas
with chilli jam

450 g (1 lb/about 6 small)
   tomatoes, blanched,
   peeled and chopped
1 chipotle chilli in adobo
   sauce (see note), plus
   1 tablespoon of sauce
½ bunch coriander
   (cilantro), plus roots,
   roughly chopped
   (reserve a few leaves
   for garnish)
1 red capsicum (pepper),
   roasted and peeled
2 tablespoons olive oil,
   plus extra for brushing
1 red onion, finely diced
4 garlic cloves, crushed
125 ml (4½ fl oz/½ cup)
   white wine
250 ml (9 fl oz/1 cup)
   chicken stock
500 g (1 lb 2 oz) piece of
   pork shoulder, bone in
sea salt and freshly ground
   black pepper
1 loaf rye sourdough, cut
   into 2 cm (¾ inch)
   thick slices

Preheat the oven to 160°C (315°F/Gas 2–3).

Place the tomato, chilli, adobo sauce, coriander and capsicum in a food processor and process until finely chopped. Set aside.

Heat the oil in a large, heavy-based, ovenproof saucepan over medium–high heat, add the onion and garlic and sauté for 2–3 minutes until translucent. Add the tomato mixture, wine and stock, and bring to the boil. Add the pork, cover, transfer to the oven and bake for 2½–3 hours until the meat is falling off the bone. Remove the pork from the pan and, when cool enough to handle, finely shred the meat from the bones. Season with salt and pepper and set aside.

Meanwhile, to make the chilli jam, place the tomato, chilli, capsicum, onion, garlic and oil in a saucepan over medium–low heat and cook for 1 hour. Add the sugar, increase the heat to medium and cook for a further hour or until the oil starts to separate from the jam. Pour into a sterilised jar and leave to cool.

Increase the oven to 200°C (400°F/Gas 6). Using a 5 cm (2 inch) round cutter, cut 25 rounds from the slices of sourdough. Lightly brush with oil, place on baking trays and bake for 10–15 minutes until toasted.

To serve, top each toasted round with 1 tablespoon of pork mixture, 1 teaspoon of chilli jam and garnish with a coriander leaf.

Note: Chipotle chillies in adobo sauce are available from Latin-American grocers and gourmet food stores. The chilli jam makes about 1½ cups and will keep refrigerated for 2–3 weeks.

450 g (1 lb/about 6 small)
    tomatoes, blanched,
    peeled and finely diced
130 g (4⅔ oz/about 5)
    long red chillies,
    seeds removed and
    finely diced
1 red capsicum (pepper),
    roasted, peeled and
    finely diced
1 onion, finely diced
4 garlic cloves, crushed
125 ml (4½ fl oz/½ cup)
    olive oil
110 g (3¾ oz/½ cup) caster
    (superfine) sugar

sweet capsicum relish

250 g (9 oz/about 3) tomatoes, blanched, peeled and finely diced

2 red capsicums (peppers), finely diced

2 onions, finely diced

3 tablespoons salt

250 ml (9 fl oz/1 cup) white vinegar

165 g (5¾ oz/¾ cup) caster (superfine) sugar

½ teaspoon smoked sweet paprika

1 teaspoon ground cumin

manchego croquettes
with sweet capsicum relish

3 tablespoons olive oil
4–6 French shallots,
    finely diced
2 garlic cloves, crushed
2 teaspoons smoked
    sweet paprika
100 g (3½ oz) butter
125 g (4½ oz) plain
    (all-purpose) flour
700 ml (24 fl oz) warm
    milk
100 g (3½ oz) manchego
    cheese, finely grated
    (see note)
sea salt and freshly
    ground black pepper
2 eggs, lightly beaten
120 g (4¼ oz/2 cups)
    panko (Japanese)
    breadcrumbs
vegetable oil, for
    deep-frying

Heat the olive oil in a frying pan over medium–high heat, add the shallots and garlic and sauté until softened and translucent. Stir in the paprika and set aside.

Melt the butter in a saucepan over medium heat, add the flour and cook for 2–3 minutes. Add the milk, a little at a time, stirring well after each addition to prevent lumps forming. Continue stirring for 5 minutes or until the sauce is thick and smooth. Add the shallot mixture and cheese and stir until melted. Season with salt and pepper. Spread onto a tray and refrigerate for 3–4 hours until set.

Meanwhile, to make the relish, place the tomato, capsicum and onion in a large bowl, sprinkle with the salt and leave for 3–4 hours. Rinse off the salt and drain well. Place in a saucepan with the vinegar, sugar, paprika and cumin over medium heat. Bring to the boil, reduce the heat and simmer for 20–30 minutes until thickened. Serve at room temperature.

Remove the croquette mixture from the refrigerator and roll single tablespoon amounts into egg-shaped balls. Dip each ball in the egg and roll in the breadcrumbs.

Heat the vegetable oil in a deep-fryer or large, heavy-based saucepan to 180°C (350°F) and deep-fry the croquettes, in batches, for 3–4 minutes until golden all over. Drain on kitchen paper.

To serve, place 2–3 croquettes in small newspaper cones or bamboo boats with the relish on the side.

Note: Manchego, a hard Spanish cheese made from sheep's milk, is available from delicatessens.

69

crab cakes
with wasabi avocado

500 g (1 lb 2 oz) cooked
   crabmeat
3 spring onions (scallions),
   chopped, plus extra
   for garnish
1 garlic clove, crushed
3 teaspoons soy sauce
1½ tablespoons chopped
   coriander (cilantro)
1 egg white
100 g (3½ oz/1¼ cups)
   fresh breadcrumbs,
   made from day-old
   bread
sea salt and freshly
   ground black pepper
vegetable oil, for
   shallow-frying
1 avocado
1 teaspoon wasabi paste
1 teaspoon lemon juice
1 teaspoon black sesame
   seeds

Combine the crabmeat, spring onion, garlic, soy sauce, coriander, egg white and breadcrumbs in a bowl and season with salt and pepper. Shape single tablespoon amounts of mixture into patties.

Heat 2 cm (¾ inch) oil in a large, heavy-based frying pan over medium heat. Cook the patties, in batches, for 1–2 minutes on each side until golden. Drain on kitchen paper and keep warm. Repeat with the remaining patties.

Mash the avocado, wasabi and lemon juice together in a small bowl and season with salt and pepper.

To serve, top each crab cake with some avocado mixture, and sprinkle with black sesame seeds and spring onion.

*empanada dough

125 ml (4½ fl oz/½ cup) warm milk

1 x 7 g (¼ oz) sachet dried yeast

1½ tablespoons caster (superfine) sugar

335 g (11¾ oz/2¼ cups) plain (all-purpose) flour, sifted

225 g (8 oz/1½ cups) polenta

2 eggs

90 g (3¼ oz/⅓ cup) sour cream

80 g (2¾ oz) butter, melted

cannellini bean
and chorizo empanadas

makes 30

1 tablespoon olive oil
½ onion, finely diced
1 teaspoon smoked
   sweet paprika
1 teaspoon ground cumin
135 g (4¾ oz) chorizo
   sausage, finely diced
2 small tomatoes,
   finely diced
125 ml (4½ fl oz/½ cup)
   chicken stock
400 g (14 oz) canned
   cannellini beans,
   drained
sea salt and freshly
   ground black pepper
¼ cup chopped coriander
   (cilantro)
olive oil spray, for greasing
250 g (9 oz/1 cup) crème
   fraîche
juice of 1 lime

To make the empanada dough, combine the milk, yeast and sugar in a bowl and leave in a warm place for 10–15 minutes until frothy. Place the flour and polenta in the bowl of an electric mixer fitted with a dough hook and make a well in the centre. Lightly beat the eggs and sour cream together, then stir in the yeast mixture. Add to the flour mixture along with the butter, and mix well to form a dough. Knead on a floured surface for 10 minutes or until smooth and elastic. Place in an oiled bowl, cover with a kitchen towel and leave in a warm place for 1½ hours or until doubled in size.

Meanwhile, heat the oil in a saucepan over medium heat, add the onion and sauté for 1–2 minutes until translucent. Stir in the spices. Add the chorizo and cook for 1 minute. Add the tomato, stock and beans, bring to the boil, reduce the heat, cover and simmer for 10 minutes. Remove from the heat and mash roughly with a fork. Season with salt and pepper and stir the coriander through.

Preheat the oven to 180°C (350°F/Gas 4). Line 2 baking trays with baking paper. Roll out the dough to 5 mm (¼ inch) thick and, using a 7 cm (2¾ inch) round cutter, cut out 30 circles. Do not re-roll the scraps. Place 1 tablespoon of filling onto one half of each circle, brush the edges with water, fold in half and press to seal. Place on the trays, spray with oil and bake for 15 minutes or until light golden.

Combine the crème fraîche and lime juice and serve alongside the empanadas.

north african tuna
and preserved lemon parcels

1 x 375 g (13 oz) can tuna in olive oil, drained
1 small red onion, finely diced
¼ cup finely chopped dill
¼ cup finely chopped flat-leaf (Italian) parsley
½ preserved lemon, flesh discarded and rind finely chopped
½ teaspoon cayenne pepper
juice of 1 lime
24 small spring roll wrappers
24 quail eggs
3 egg yolks, lightly beaten
vegetable oil, for deep-frying

Combine the tuna, onion, dill, parsley, preserved lemon, cayenne pepper and lime juice in a bowl.

Lay a spring roll wrapper on a surface. Keep the rest of the wrappers covered with a damp kitchen towel to prevent them from drying out. Place 1 tablespoon of mixture in the centre of the wrapper. Make a well in the centre of the mixture, then break a quail egg into the well. Brush the edges of the wrapper with the lightly beaten egg yolk, fold the edge closest to you up over the mix, then fold the opposite edge over the top. Brush the sides with egg yolk, then fold both sides into the middle to form a well-sealed square. Repeat with the remaining wrappers, mixture and quail eggs.

Heat the oil in a deep-fryer or large, heavy-based saucepan over medium heat to 180°C (350°F). Deep-fry the parcels, in batches, for 3–4 minutes until golden. Drain on kitchen paper.

pizzettes with goat's milk camembert and pickled walnut

250 g (9 oz) goat's milk
  camembert cheese,
  thinly sliced
24 cherry tomatoes, sliced
walnut oil, for drizzling
  (see note)
8–10 pickled walnuts,
  sliced (see note)
¼ cup flat-leaf (Italian)
  parsley, finely shredded

PIZZA DOUGH
400 g (14 oz/2⅔ cups)
  plain (all-purpose) flour,
  sifted
1 x 7 g (¼ oz) sachet dried
  yeast
2 tablespoons olive oil
1 tablespoon honey
pinch of salt

To make the pizza dough, place all of the ingredients and 250 ml (9 fl oz/1 cup) warm water in the bowl of an electric mixer fitted with a dough hook, combine well, then knead on a floured surface for 10 minutes or until smooth and elastic. Place in an oiled bowl, cover with a kitchen towel and leave in a warm place for 1 hour or until doubled in size.

Preheat the oven to 220°C (425°F/Gas 7). Lightly oil 2 baking trays. Knock back the dough and divide into 24 pieces. Roll each into a ball, place on a floured surface, cover with a kitchen towel and leave for 20–30 minutes until doubled in size. Press each ball into a 7 cm (2¾ inch) round and place onto the trays. Divide the camembert among the rounds, top with 3 slices of tomato and drizzle with a little walnut oil. Bake for 10–15 minutes until golden.

To serve, top each pizzette with a slice of pickled walnut and some parsley.

Note: Walnut oil and pickled walnuts are available from gourmet food stores. Walnut oil is very strongly flavoured, so only use a little.

smoked ham and
cheddar quichettes with green tomato pickle

1 x quantity shortcrust
    pastry (see page 25)
250 g (9 oz) double-
    smoked ham, finely
    diced
200 g (7 oz) cheddar
    cheese, finely grated
2 large eggs
3 tablespoons pouring
    (single) cream
fresh thyme leaves, to
    garnish

GREEN TOMATO PICKLE
500 g (1 lb 2 oz) green
    tomatoes, finely diced
2 small onions, finely
    diced
3 tablespoons salt
1 teaspoon yellow
    mustard seeds
¼ teaspoon ground
    turmeric
1 cinnamon stick
6 cloves
200 ml (7 fl oz) white
    vinegar
150 g (5½ oz) caster
    (superfine) sugar

Make the shortcrust pastry dough (see page 25) and refrigerate for 1 hour.

Meanwhile, to make the pickle, place the tomato and onion in a large bowl, sprinkle with the salt and leave for 3–4 hours. Rinse off the salt and drain well. Place in a saucepan with the remaining ingredients. Bring to the boil over medium heat, reduce the heat and simmer for 30–40 minutes until thickened. Pour into a sterilised jar and leave to cool.

Preheat the oven to 180°C (350°F/Gas 4). Lightly grease twenty-four 6 cm x 2 cm (2½ inch x ¾ inch) fluted or plain tartlet tins. Roll out the pastry to 5 mm (¼ inch) thick and, using an 8 cm (3¼ inch) round cutter, cut out 24 circles. Press each circle into the tins, trimming excess pastry. Place on baking trays and refrigerate for 30 minutes. To blind bake the cases, line them with baking paper and fill with dried beans, rice or baking weights. Bake for 15–20 minutes, remove the beans and paper and bake for a further 10–15 minutes until golden and cooked through. Remove and set aside to cool in tins.

Divide the ham and cheese between the cases. Whisk the eggs and cream together in a jug and pour into the cases. Bake for 15–20 minutes until golden and set. Cool slightly and remove from the tins.

To serve, top each quiche with 1 teaspoon of pickle and garnish with thyme leaves.

78

Note: The green tomato pickle makes 2 cups and will keep refrigerated for 4–6 weeks.

char-grilled scallops
wrapped in prosciutto

makes 24

3 tablespoons olive oil
1 tablespoon lemon juice
2 garlic cloves, crushed
1 small red chilli, finely diced
1 teaspoon finely grated lemon zest
1 teaspoon chopped rosemary
sea salt and freshly ground black pepper
24 scallops, roe removed
12 thin slices prosciutto, halved lengthways
shredded lettuce, to serve

Whisk the oil, lemon juice, garlic, chilli, lemon zest and rosemary together in a bowl. Season with salt and pepper. Add the scallops and toss to coat well.

Wrap a piece of prosciutto around each scallop and secure with a toothpick.

Preheat a barbecue or char-grill pan to medium–high. Cook the scallops for 1–2 minutes on each side until just cooked.

Serve on a bed of shredded lettuce.

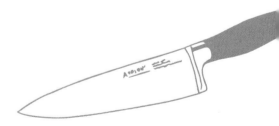

chicken pizzettes
with rosella paste and macadamia nuts

1 x quantity pizza dough
(see page 77)
1 x 180 g (6½ oz) skinless
chicken breast fillet
sea salt and freshly
ground black pepper
2 tablespoons olive oil
200 g (7 oz) goat's curd
35 g (1¼ oz/¼ cup)
chopped toasted
macadamia nuts
fresh micro herbs, for
garnish

ROSELLA PASTE
500 g (1 lb 2 oz) frozen
rosella flowers with
seeds (see note)
1 small apple, peeled,
cored and chopped
330 g (11¾ oz/1½ cups)
caster (superfine) sugar

Make the pizza dough (see page 77) and leave in a warm place for 1 hour.

Meanwhile, to make the rosella paste, remove the seeds from the rosella flowers. Roughly chop the flowers, place in a saucepan and set aside. Place the seeds in a separate saucepan, cover with water and bring to the boil, reduce the heat and simmer for 30 minutes. Strain the liquid, discarding the seeds, and add the liquid to the flowers. Add the apple, cover with water and simmer for 20 minutes. Add the sugar and cook for a further 20 minutes or until the paste is thick. Pour into a sterilised jar and leave to cool.

Preheat the oven to 190°C (375°F/Gas 5). Season the chicken with salt and pepper. Heat the oil in an ovenproof frying pan over medium–high heat, add the chicken and cook for 1 minute on each side or until browned, then roast for 10–15 minutes until cooked through. Cool, then cut into small dice.

Increase the oven to 220°C (425°F/Gas 7). Lightly oil 2 baking trays. Knock back the dough and divide into 24 pieces. Roll each into a ball, place on a floured surface, cover with a kitchen towel and leave for 20–30 minutes until doubled in size. Press each ball into a 7 cm (2¾ inch) round and place onto the trays. Spread each with 1 teaspoon of goat's curd and bake for 10–15 minutes until the bases are crisp and golden. Top each with some chicken and 1 teaspoon of rosella paste, sprinkle with the nuts and garnish with the herbs.

Note: Rosella flowers are available from health food stores and gourmet food stores. The rosella paste makes about 500 ml (18 fl oz/2 cups). This can be made the day before and will keep refrigerated for 6 months.

zucchini & haloumi
fritters with roasted capsicum salsa

makes 24

1 small red capsicum
   (pepper)
1 tablespoon chopped
   flat-leaf (Italian) parsley
1 tablespoon lemon juice
350 g (12 oz/about 3)
   zucchini (courgettes)
250 g (9 oz/2½ cups)
   grated haloumi cheese
3 spring onions (scallions),
   chopped
75 g (2¾ oz/½ cup) plain
   (all-purpose) flour
2 eggs, lightly beaten
1 tablespoon chopped dill
sea salt and freshly
   ground black pepper
olive oil, for shallow-frying

Preheat the oven to 180°C (350°F/Gas 4). Place the capsicum on a baking tray and roast for 20 minutes or until the skin has blackened. Transfer to a bowl, cover with plastic wrap and leave for 10 minutes. Remove the skin and seeds. Cut the capsicum into thin strips and place in a bowl with the parsley and lemon juice. Set aside until required.

Coarsely grate the zucchini. Wrap in a kitchen towel and wring out to remove excess moisture. Place in a bowl, add the haloumi, spring onion, flour, egg and dill, season with salt and pepper and stir to combine.

Heat 2 cm (¾ inch) oil in a large, heavy-based frying pan over medium heat, add single tablespoon amounts of the zucchini mixture, flatten out slightly and cook for 1–2 minutes on each side until golden. Drain on kitchen paper and keep warm. Repeat with the remaining mixture.

To serve, top each fritter with a spoonful of the capsicum salsa.

85

tostadas with
chipotle chicken and guacamole

1 x 180 g (6½ oz) skinless
   chicken breast fillet
2 tablespoons olive oil
1 small onion, thinly sliced
1 chipotle chilli in adobo
   sauce (see note),
   seeds removed
250 g (9 oz/1 cup) canned
   diced tomatoes
250 ml (9 fl oz/1 cup)
   chicken stock
1 tablespoon tomato
   paste (concentrated
   purée)
1 cup chopped coriander
   (cilantro), plus leaves,
   for garnish
finely grated zest and
   juice of 1 lime
sea salt and freshly
   ground black pepper
1 ripe avocado
2–3 tablespoons
   lemon juice
5–6 large round
   corn tortillas
vegetable oil, for
   deep-frying

Bring a saucepan of water to the boil, reduce the heat to medium–low, add the chicken and poach gently for 15 minutes or until cooked through. Drain and, when cool enough to handle, finely shred.

Heat the olive oil in a saucepan over medium heat, add the onion and sauté for 2–3 minutes until softened and translucent. Add the chilli, tomato, stock, tomato paste and chicken. Bring to the boil, reduce the heat, cover and simmer for 10 minutes. Remove the lid and cook for 10–15 minutes until the sauce has thickened. Stir in the coriander, lime zest and juice. Season with salt and pepper, and keep warm.

Combine the avocado and lemon juice in a bowl and mash together with a fork. Set aside.

Using a 5 cm (2 inch) round cutter, cut out 20 rounds from the tortillas. Heat the vegetable oil in a deep-fryer or large, heavy-based saucepan to 180°C (350°F) and deep-fry the tortilla rounds, in batches, for 2 minutes or until crisp. Drain on kitchen paper.

To serve, top each tortilla round with a smear of mashed avocado and 1 tablespoon of chicken mixture and garnish with a coriander leaf.

Note: Chipotle chillies in adobo sauce are available from Latin-American grocers and gourmet food stores.

smoked trout, lime
and quail egg tartlets

12 quail eggs
2 tablespoons crème
    fraîche
2 tablespoons lime juice
finely grated zest of 1 lime
250 g (9 oz) smoked trout,
    flaked, skin and bones
    discarded
fresh chervil, to garnish
Cyprus black sea salt
    (see note)

SHORTCRUST PASTRY
300 g (10½ oz/2 cups)
    plain (all-purpose) flour
120 g (4¼ oz) cold
    unsalted butter, cubed
pinch of salt
2 egg yolks

To make the shortcrust pastry, place the flour, butter and salt in a food processor and pulse until the mixture resembles breadcrumbs. Add the egg yolks and 80 ml (2½ fl oz/⅓ cup) cold water and pulse again until just starting to come together. Knead on a floured surface to bring together, shape into a disc, wrap in plastic wrap and refrigerate for 1 hour.

Preheat the oven to 180°C (350°F/Gas 4). Lightly grease twenty-four 6 cm x 1 cm (2½ inch x ½ inch) fluted or plain tartlet tins.

Roll out the pastry to 5 mm (¼ inch) thick and, using an 8 cm (3¼ inch) round cutter, cut out 24 circles. Press each circle into the tins, trimming excess pastry. Place on baking trays and refrigerate for 30 minutes. To blind bake the cases, line them with baking paper and fill with dried beans, rice or baking weights. Bake for 15–20 minutes, remove the beans and paper and bake for a further 10–15 minutes until golden and cooked through. Leave to cool in tins, then turn out.

Bring a large saucepan of water to the boil. Using a spoon, carefully place the quail eggs into the pan. Bring back to the boil and cook for 1½ minutes. Drain and refresh in cold water. When cool enough to handle, peel and halve lengthways.

Combine the crème fraîche, and lime juice and zest in a bowl. Gently fold in the trout. Divide the mixture between the pastry cases, top each with a quail-egg half, garnish with chervil and sprinkle with the black salt.

Note: Cyprus black sea salt is available from gourmet food stores.

89

mini duck pies
with broad bean mash

2 tablespoons olive oil
3 duck marylands,
   trimmed
2 French shallots, finely
   chopped
2 garlic cloves, crushed
50 g (1¾ oz) bacon, finely
   diced
1 small carrot, finely diced
1 stick celery, finely diced
3–4 sprigs thyme
2 fresh bay leaves
185 ml (6 fl oz/¾ cup)
   red wine
375 ml (13 fl oz/1½ cups)
   beef stock
80 g (2¾ oz/¼ cup)
   redcurrant jelly
1 x quantity shortcrust
   pastry (see page 89)
sea salt and freshly
   ground black pepper
2 potatoes, roughly
   chopped
30 g (1 oz) butter
300 g (10½ oz/3 cups)
   blanched and peeled
   broad beans

Preheat the oven to 170°C (325°F/Gas 3). Heat the oil in a large, heavy-based, ovenproof saucepan over medium-high heat, add the duck and brown on each side. Remove from the pan. Add the shallots and garlic to the pan and sauté for 1–2 minutes until softened and translucent. Add the bacon and cook for 2 minutes. Add the carrot, celery and herbs and cook for 4–5 minutes until softened. Stir in the wine, stock and jelly. Bring to the boil, arrange the duck on top, cover, transfer to the oven and bake for 1½ hours or until the meat is falling off the bones.

Meanwhile, make the shortcrust pastry dough (see page 89) and refrigerate for 1 hour.

Remove the duck from the sauce. Place the sauce over medium-high heat and cook for 10 minutes or until thickened. Remove the thyme sprigs. Discard the skin from the duck and shred the meat from the bones. Stir the duck meat back into the sauce and season with salt and pepper. Cool.

Place the potato in a saucepan of water, bring to the boil and cook for 10 minutes or until tender. Drain, add the butter and mash until smooth. Add the broad beans and roughly mash, then season with salt and pepper.

Increase the oven to 190°C (375°F/Gas 5). Lightly grease twenty 6 cm x 2.5 cm (2½ inch x 1 inch) pie tins. Roll out the pastry to 5 mm (¼ inch) thick and, using an 8 cm (3¼ inch) cutter, cut out 20 circles. Press each circle into the tins, trimming excess pastry. Divide the duck mixture between the tins, top with the mash and bake for 20–25 minutes until the pastry is golden and crisp. Cool slightly in the tins, then remove using a butter knife.

*curry powder

- 1 tablespoon long-grain rice
- 1 cinnamon stick
- 3 tablespoons coriander
  seeds
- 3 tablespoons fennel seeds
- 1 tablespoon cumin seeds
- ½ teaspoon cardamom
  seeds
- ½ teaspoon black
  peppercorns
- 5 cloves
- 8–10 fresh curry leaves
  (see note)
- 2 dried red chillies

sri lankan goat
curry turnovers

3 tablespoons olive oil

500 g (1 lb 2 oz) piece of goat shoulder, cut into large pieces

1½ small onions, finely diced

2 garlic cloves, crushed

30 g (1 oz) ginger, finely chopped

1 sprig curry leaves, leaves removed (see note)

¼ teaspoon ground turmeric

2 cinnamon sticks

1 stalk lemongrass, cut into 4 cm (1½ inch) lengths and bruised

4 small tomatoes, finely diced

1 tablespoon tomato paste (concentrated purée)

sea salt and freshly ground black pepper

1.5 kg (3 lb 5 oz) good-quality pre-rolled butter puff pastry

2 eggs, lightly beaten

To make the curry powder, heat a frying pan over medium heat, add the rice and toast until lightly browned. Transfer to a bowl. Toast the remaining spices, in batches, until browned and fragrant and add to the rice. Cool, then place in a spice grinder and grind to a powder.

Preheat the oven to 180°C (350°F/Gas 4).

Heat 2 tablespoons of the oil in a large, heavy-based ovenproof saucepan over medium–high heat. Add the goat and brown all over. Remove from the pan. Add the remaining oil along with the onion, garlic and ginger, and sauté for 2–3 minutes until softened and translucent. Add the curry leaves, turmeric, cinnamon, lemongrass and 3 tablespoons of the curry powder and cook for 1 minute or until fragrant. Stir in the tomato, tomato paste and 375 ml (13 fl oz/1½ cups) water. Add the goat and juices to the pan, bring to the boil, cover, transfer to the oven and bake for 1½ hours or until tender. Break up the meat and season with salt and pepper. Cool.

Increase the oven to 220°C (425°F/Gas 7). Line 2 baking trays with baking paper. Using an 8 cm (3¼ inch) round cutter, cut out 40 circles from the pastry. Place 1 teaspoon of goat mixture onto one half of each circle. Brush the edges with water, fold in half and press to seal. Place on the trays, brush with the egg and bake for 15 minutes or until golden.

Note: Fresh curry leaves are available from Indian and Asian grocers. The curry powder will keep for 2–3 months in a sealed container.

93

saffron chicken
pies

3 tablespoons olive oil
3 French shallots, roughly
    chopped
4 garlic cloves, bruised
1 teaspoon saffron
    threads
¼ teaspoon ground
    turmeric
1 teaspoon ground ginger
1 teaspoon ground
    cinnamon, plus extra
    for dusting
900 g (2 lb/about 4)
    skinless chicken thighs,
    bone in
2 eggs, lightly beaten
¼ cup finely chopped
    flat-leaf (Italian) parsley
¼ cup finely chopped
    coriander (cilantro)
sea salt and freshly
    ground black pepper
20 sheets filo pastry
melted butter, for
    brushing
icing (confectioners')
    sugar, for dusting

Heat the oil in a saucepan over medium–low heat, add the shallots, garlic and spices, and sauté for 1 minute. Add the chicken and cook for 3 minutes or until browned all over. Add 375 ml (13 fl oz/1½ cups) water, cover, reduce the heat and simmer for 1–1½ hours until the meat is falling off the bone.

Meanwhile, to make the almond filling, heat the oil in a frying pan over medium–low heat, add the almonds and cook until golden. Drain on kitchen paper and cool, then process with the sugar in a food processor until fine crumbs form.

Remove the chicken from the pan and, when cool enough to handle, shred the meat from the bones. Combine the meat with the egg and herbs and season with salt and pepper.

Preheat the oven to 190°C (375°F/Gas 5). Line 2 baking trays with baking paper. Lay a sheet of filo on a surface. Keep the rest covered with a damp kitchen towel to prevent it from drying out. Brush half the sheet generously with the butter and fold in half. Brush with more butter and fold in half again. Trim to make a square. Place 1 tablespoon of chicken mixture in the centre and top with 1 teaspoon of filling. Brush the edges with butter and fold one edge up over the mix, then fold the opposite edge over the top. Brush the sides with butter and fold into the middle to form a well-sealed square. Place on a tray. Repeat with the remaining filo, mixture and filling. Bake for 15–20 minutes until golden.

To serve, dust the pies lightly with icing sugar and cinnamon.

*almond filling

3 tablespoons olive oil
80 g (2¾ oz/½ cup)
  blanched almonds
1 tablespoon caster
  (superfine) sugar

pandan chicken
and black bean parcels

1 tablespoon salted black
   beans, soaked in water,
   drained and finely
   chopped (see note)
1 tablespoon chilli bean
   paste (see note)
1 tablespoon kecap manis
500 g (1 lb 2 oz/about 5)
   skinless chicken
   thigh fillets
20 pandan leaves
   (see note)

Combine the salted black beans, chilli bean paste and kecap manis in a shallow bowl. Cut each thigh fillet into 4 evenly-sized pieces. Add to the salted black bean mixture and coat well. Refrigerate for 1 hour to marinate.

Preheat the oven to 180°C (350°F/Gas 4).

Lay the pandan leaves out on a surface. Place 1 piece of chicken at the end of each leaf and roll up into a triangle to enclose. Secure with a toothpick and place on a baking tray. Bake for 10–15 minutes until cooked through, turning once.

Note: Salted black beans, chilli bean paste and pandan leaves are available from Chinese or Thai grocers.

97

barramundi burgers
with lemon myrtle mayo

1 x quantity pepperberry
    mayo (see page 101),
    substitute ½ tablespoon
    ground lemon myrtle
    (see note) for
    pepperberry
600 g (1 lb 5 oz) skinless
    barramundi fillets, cut
    into pieces
finely grated zest of
    1 lemon
sea salt and freshly
    ground black pepper
plain (all-purpose) flour,
    for dusting
2 eggs, lightly beaten
120 g (4¼ oz/2 cups)
    panko (Japanese)
    breadcrumbs
80 ml (2½ fl oz/⅓ cup)
    olive oil

BURGER BUNS
300 g (10½ oz/2 cups)
    strong bread flour,
    sifted
1 tablespoon dried yeast
1 teaspoon salt
2 teaspoons ground
    lemon myrtle (see note)
3 tablespoons olive oil

To make the buns, place the flour, yeast, salt and 1½ tespoons lemon myrtle in the bowl of an electric mixer fitted with a dough hook and make a well in the centre. Add the oil and 170 ml (5½ fl oz/⅔ cup) warm water and mix on low speed to combine. Knead on a floured surface for 15 minutes or until the dough is smooth and elastic. Place in an oiled bowl, cover with a kitchen towel and leave in a warm place for 45 minutes or until doubled in size.

Meanwhile, make the lemon myrtle mayo (see page 101, substituting lemon myrtle for pepperberry).

Preheat the oven to 250°C (500°F/Gas 9). Line 2 baking trays with baking paper. Divide the dough into 20 pieces. Roll each into a ball and place on the trays. Press lightly to flatten, sprinkle with salt and remaining lemon myrtle and drizzle with the oil. Leave in a warm place for 30 minutes or until doubled in size. Bake for 15–20 minutes until golden.

Roughly chop the fish in a food processor. Transfer to a bowl, combine with the lemon zest, season with salt and pepper, and shape into 20 patties. Dust each in flour, dip in the egg and press in the breadcrumbs.

Heat the oil in a large frying pan over medium–high heat and cook the patties, in batches, for 2–3 minutes on each side until cooked through.

To serve, halve each bun, place a patty on the bottom halves, top with a dollop of mayonnaise, sandwich with the tops and secure with a toothpick.

Note: Ground lemon myrtle is available from specialty Indigenous food suppliers. The mayonnaise makes 1½ cups and will keep refrigerated for 2–3 days.

fig galettes with
jamón and
pepperberry mayo

1 x quantity shortcrust
pastry (see page 102)
12 small figs, halved
olive oil, for drizzling
12 thin slices (about 120 g/
4¼ oz) jamón Ibérico,
halved crossways
flat-leaf (Italian) parsley
leaves, for garnish

PEPPERBERRY
MAYO
1 egg
1 egg yolk
2 teaspoons Dijon
mustard
300 ml (10½ fl oz)
vegetable oil
2 tablespoons lemon juice
1 tablespoon ground
pepperberry (see note)
sea salt

Make the shortcrust pastry dough (see page 102) and refrigerate for 1 hour.

Meanwhile, to make the pepperberry mayo, whisk the egg, egg yolk and mustard together in a large bowl. While whisking, add the oil in a thin continuous stream until it is all added and the mayonnaise is thick. Whisk in the lemon juice and pepperberry, and season with salt. Cover closely with plastic wrap and refrigerate until required.

Preheat the oven to 190°C (375°F/Gas 5). Line 2 baking trays with baking paper. Roll out the pastry to 5 mm (¼ inch) thick and, using a 10 cm (4 inch) round cutter, cut out 24 circles. Place a fig half, cut side up, on each circle. Bring the pastry up around the fig to encase and pleat the edges to secure. Place on the trays and drizzle with the oil. Bake for 15–20 minutes until golden.

To serve, top each galette with a slice of jamón and a dollop of mayonnaise. and garnish with the parsley.

Note: Ground pepperberry is available from specialty Indigenous food suppliers. The mayonnaise makes 1½ cups and will keep refrigerated for 2–3 days.

beef and sherry
pastries

3 tablespoons olive oil
350 g (12 oz) stewing beef,
  cut into 2 cm (¾ inch)
  dice
2 French shallots, finely
  diced
2 garlic cloves, crushed
1 small carrot, finely diced
½ leek, white part only,
  finely diced
2 fresh bay leaves
250 g (9 oz/about 3 small)
  tomatoes, finely diced
125 ml (4½ fl oz/½ cup)
  fino (dry) sherry
1 tablespoon plain
  (all-purpose) flour
1 tablespoon tomato
  paste (concentrated
  purée)
sea salt and freshly
  ground black pepper
1 egg, lightly beaten

SHORTCRUST PASTRY
300 g (10½ oz/2 cups)
  plain (all-purpose) flour
120 g (4¼ oz) cold
  unsalted butter, cubed
pinch of salt
2 egg yolks

Heat 2 tablespoons of the oil in a large, heavy-based saucepan over medium–high heat, add the beef and brown all over. Remove the beef from the pan. Add the remaining oil, shallots and garlic and sauté for 2–3 minutes until softened and translucent. Add the carrot, leek and bay leaves and cook for 2 minutes. Return the beef to the pan. Add the tomato, sherry and 60 ml (2¼ fl oz/¼ cup) water, bring to the boil, reduce the heat, cover and simmer for 1½ hours or until the beef is fork-tender.

Meanwhile, to make the pastry, place the flour, butter and salt in a food processor and pulse until the mixture resembles breadcrumbs. Add the egg yolks and 80 ml (2½ fl oz/⅓ cup) cold water and pulse again until just starting to come together. Knead on a floured surface to bring together, shape into a disc, wrap in plastic wrap and refrigerate for 1 hour.

Preheat the oven to 200°C (400°F/Gas 6). Line 2 baking trays with baking paper.

Combine the flour and 2 tablespoons water to make a paste. Add to the beef with the tomato paste. Cook, uncovered, for 10–15 minutes until the sauce has thickened. Season with salt and pepper, and cool.

Roll out the pastry to 5 mm (¼ inch) thick and, using a 10 cm (4 inch) round cutter, cut out 30 circles. Place 1 tablespoon of mixture in the centre of each pastry round. Bring the 2 sides up to meet at the top and pinch together, making a frill. Place on the trays, brush with the egg and bake for 20–25 minutes until golden.

caramelised leek
and artichoke scones

makes 12

40 g (1½ oz) butter
½ leek, white part only, finely diced
1 tablespoon soft brown sugar
2 marinated artichoke hearts, roughly chopped
500 g (1 lb 2 oz/3⅓ cups) self-raising (self-rising) flour
2 teaspoons baking powder
pinch of salt
100 g (3½ oz) cold unsalted butter, cubed
150 ml (5 fl oz) buttermilk

Preheat the oven to 220°C (425°F/Gas 7). Line a baking tray with baking paper.

Heat the butter in a frying pan over medium heat, add the leek and cook for 5 minutes or until softened and golden. Add the sugar and cook for 1 minute. Stir the artichoke through and leave to cool.

Place the flour, baking powder, salt and cubed butter in a food processor and pulse until the mixture resembles breadcrumbs. Add the buttermilk and 150 ml (5 fl oz) cold water and pulse again until the mixture just starts to come together. Tip onto a floured surface, add the leek mixture and bring together quickly with your hands, making sure to not overwork the dough. Pat the dough out to 2 cm (¾ inch) thick. Using a 4 cm (1½ inch) round cutter, cut out 12 rounds and arrange so they are touching on the tray to make a neat 3 x 4 rectangle. Bake for 15 minutes or until light golden.

cauliflower galettes
with taleggio and walnuts

250 g (9 oz) cauliflower,
cut into small florets
2 tablespoons olive oil
3 French shallots, finely
diced
1 teaspoon caraway
seeds
sea salt and freshly
ground black pepper
250 g (9 oz) Taleggio
cheese, thinly sliced
walnut oil, for drizzling
(see note)
30 g (1 oz/¼ cup)
chopped walnuts
flat-leaf (Italian) parsley
leaves, to garnish

SHORTCRUST PASTRY
300 g (10½ oz/2 cups)
plain (all-purpose) flour
120 g (4¼ oz) cold
unsalted butter, cubed
pinch of salt
2 egg yolks

To make the pastry, place the flour, butter and salt in a food processor and pulse until the mixture resembles breadcrumbs. Add the yolks and 80 ml (2½ fl oz/⅓ cup) cold water and pulse again until just starting to come together. Knead on a floured surface to bring together, shape into a disc, wrap in plastic wrap and refrigerate for 1 hour.

Meanwhile, bring a saucepan of water to the boil, add the cauliflower and cook for 3–4 minutes until tender. Drain and refresh in cold water. Heat the olive oil in a frying pan over medium heat, add the shallots and sauté for 1–2 minutes until softened and translucent. Add the caraway seeds and cauliflower and cook for 3 minutes. Season with salt and pepper. Leave to cool slightly.

Preheat the oven to 190°C (375°F/Gas 5). Line 2 baking trays with baking paper. Roll out the pastry to 5 mm (¼ inch) thick and, using a 10 cm (4 inch) round cutter, cut out 24 circles. Divide the cheese between the circles and top with the cauliflower mixture. Bring the pastry up around the filling to encase and pleat the edges to secure. Place on the trays and bake for 15–20 minutes until golden.

To serve, drizzle over a little walnut oil, and garnish with the walnuts and parsley leaves.

Note: Walnut oil is available from gourmet food stores. It is very strongly flavoured so only use a little.

crumpets with goat's
curd and lavender honey

makes about 24

½ teaspoon dried yeast
3 teaspoons caster
   (superfine) sugar
125 ml (4½ fl oz/½ cup)
   milk
150 g (5½ oz/1 cup) plain
   (all-purpose) flour, sifted
pinch of salt
¼ teaspoon bicarbonate
   of soda (baking soda),
   sifted
1 egg, separated
vegetable oil spray
250 g (9 oz) goat's curd
lavender honey (see
   note), to serve

Combine the yeast, 1 teaspoon of sugar and
1 tablespoon warm water in a bowl and leave in a
warm place for 10–15 minutes until frothy.

Heat the milk with 80 ml (2½ fl oz/⅓ cup) water in
a saucepan over low heat.

Place the flour, salt and bicarbonate of soda in a large
bowl and make a well in the centre. Place the egg yolk
and remaining sugar in a separate bowl and whisk
together until pale and fluffy. Whisk in the yeast mixture
and warm milk. Mix into the dry ingredients to make a
batter, stirring well to make sure there are no lumps.

Whisk the egg white until stiff peaks form, then gently
fold in the batter.

Heat a large non-stick frying pan over medium–high
heat. Spray the pan with vegetable oil and add single
tablespoon amounts of batter to the pan, cooking
4 crumpets at a time. Cook for 2–3 minutes until the
edges start to dry and holes start to form in the top, then
flip over and cook for a further minute. Remove from the
pan and keep warm under a kitchen towel. Repeat with
the remaining batter.

To serve, top each crumpet with a heaped teaspoon
of goat's curd and drizzle with the honey.

Note: Lavender honey is available
from gourmet food stores.

raspberry cupcakes

with white chocolate ganache

makes 48

48 fresh raspberries, plus
  extra to garnish
  (optional)
250 g (9 oz) white
  chocolate
120 g (4¼ oz) unsalted
  butter
85 g (3 oz) caster
  (superfine) sugar
125 ml (4½ fl oz/½ cup)
  milk
125 g (4½ oz) plain
  (all-purpose) flour
½ teaspoon baking
  powder
1 egg, lightly beaten
½ teaspoon natural vanilla
  extract

WHITE CHOCOLATE
  GANACHE
180 g (6⅓ oz) white
  chocolate, finely
  chopped
400 ml (14 fl oz) pouring
  (single) cream

To make the ganache, place the chocolate and cream in the top of a double boiler over medium heat and stir until melted and smooth. Transfer to a bowl and refrigerate for 20 minutes. Remove and stir, then refrigerate for a further 20 minutes. Repeat the process twice more. (At this point, the ganache can be covered and refrigerated overnight.)

Meanwhile, preheat the oven to 150°C (300°F/Gas 2). Line forty-eight 30 ml (1 fl oz/⅛ cup) capacity mini-muffin holes with paper cases and place 1 raspberry in the base of each.

Finely chop 150 g (5½ oz) of the white chocolate. Place in the top of a double boiler over medium heat with the butter, sugar and milk, and stir until melted and smooth. Leave to cool for 15 minutes.

Sift the flour and baking powder together into a large bowl. Add the chocolate mixture and stir to combine. Add the egg and vanilla extract and mix well. (The batter should be quite runny.) Transfer to a jug and pour into the cases, filling them three-quarters full. Bake for 11–12 minutes until cooked. Cool in the tins for 3–5 minutes, then turn out onto wire racks to cool completely.

Transfer the ganache to the bowl of an electric mixer and beat on medium speed for 1–2 minutes until soft peaks form. Transfer to a large piping bag fitted with a small star nozzle and pipe swirls of ganache onto each cupcake. Top each with a raspberry, if desired, and shave remaining white chocolate over cupcakes using a vegetable peeler.

113

raspberry macarons
with white chocolate

Makes about 30

120 g (4¼ oz) almond meal
   (ground almonds)
220 g (7¾ oz) icing
   (confectioners') sugar
110 g (3¾ oz) egg white
30 g (1 oz) caster
   (superfine) sugar
2 teaspoons natural
   raspberry extract
pink food colouring, paste
   or powdered is
   preferable

WHITE CHOCOLATE
   GANACHE
120 g (4¼ oz) white
   chocolate, chopped
2½ tablespoons pouring
   (single) cream
2 teaspoons natural
   raspberry extract
3 teaspoons raspberry
   jam

Line 2 baking trays with baking paper. Process the almond meal and icing sugar in a food processor until combined, then sift twice. Place the egg white in the bowl of an electric mixer and beat on medium speed until frothy, then increase the speed while gradually adding the caster sugar. Continue beating until stiff peaks form, then mix in the raspberry extract and enough colouring for desired effect. Fold one-third into the almond mixture and combine well. Gently fold the remaining egg white mixture through; it should be glossy and thick, not thin and runny.

Transfer to a piping bag fitted with a 5 mm (¼ inch) plain nozzle and pipe 3 cm (1¼ inch) circles about 3 cm (1¼ inches) apart onto the trays. Leave at room temperature for 1–6 hours (depending on the humidity) until a crust forms; the macarons should be not sticky to the touch.

Preheat the oven to 140°C (275°F/Gas 1). Bake the macarons for 15–18 minutes until they rise slightly. Immediately slide the macarons and paper off the trays and onto wire racks to cool completely.

Meanwhile, to make the ganache, place the chocolate and cream in the top of a double boiler over medium heat and stir until melted and smooth. Refrigerate for 25–35 minutes until firm but pliable. Add the raspberry extract and jam and mix well.

Transfer to a small piping bag fitted with a 1 cm (½ inch) plain nozzle and pipe 1-teaspoon amounts onto half of the macarons. Sandwich with the remaining macarons.

114

*dulce de leche
frosting
125 g (4½ oz) unsalted
  butter, at room
  temperature
375 g (13 oz/3 cups) icing
  (confectioners') sugar
3 tablespoons pouring
  (single) cream
2 teaspoons natural vanilla
  extract
125 ml (4½ fl oz/½ cup)
  dulce de leche (see note)

dulce de leche
cupcakes

makes 42

185 g (6½ oz/1¼ cups) plain (all-purpose) flour

¾ teaspoon baking powder

2½ teaspoons ground cinnamon, plus extra for dusting

125 g (4½ oz) unsalted butter, at room temperature

185 g (6½ oz/1 cup lightly packed) soft brown sugar

2 eggs

125 ml (4½ fl oz/½ cup) buttermilk

1 teaspoon natural vanilla extract

125 ml (4½ fl oz/½ cup) dulce de leche (see note)

Preheat oven to 180°C (350°F/Gas 4). Line forty-two 30 ml (1 fl oz/⅛ cup) capacity mini-muffin holes with paper cases.

To make the cupcakes, sift the flour, baking powder and cinnamon together into a bowl.

Place the butter and sugar in the bowl of an electric mixer and beat on medium speed for 2–3 minutes until light and creamy. Add the eggs, one at a time, beating well after each addition. Add the flour mixture in 2 batches, alternating with the buttermilk, scraping down the sides of the bowl as required. Beat in the vanilla extract.

Transfer the batter to a large piping bag fitted with a 1 cm (½ inch) plain nozzle and pipe into the cases, filling them three-quarters full. Bake for 10–12 minutes until lightly golden and they spring back lightly to the touch. Cool in the tins for 1–2 minutes, then turn out onto wire racks to cool completely.

Fill a piping bag fitted with a small plain nozzle tip with the dulce de leche. Insert the nozzle into each cupcake and pipe a little dulce de leche into the centre.

To make the frosting, place the butter, icing sugar, cream and vanilla extract in the bowl of an electric mixer and beat on medium speed for 3–4 minutes. Increase the speed to high and beat until light and creamy. Reduce the speed, add the dulce de leche and beat to combine. Transfer to a large piping bag fitted with a small star nozzle and pipe onto the cupcakes. Dust with the extra cinnamon.

Note: Dulce de leche is available from Latin American grocers and gourmet food shops.

makes 30

lemon cheesecakes
with blueberry sauce

90 g (3¼ oz) gingersnap
biscuits, crushed
40 g (1½ oz) unsalted
butter, melted
250 g (9 oz/1 cup) cream
cheese, at room
temperature
110 g (3¾ oz/½ cup)
caster (superfine) sugar
1 egg
1½ tablespoons plain
(all-purpose) flour
1 tablespoon lemon juice
finely grated zest of
1 lemon
150 g (5½ oz/1 cup) fresh
blueberries

BLUEBERRY SAUCE
150 g (5½ oz/1 cup) fresh
blueberries
55 g (2 oz/¼ cup) caster
(superfine) sugar
3 tablespoons lemon juice
1 tablespoon blueberry
jam

Preheat the oven to 150°C (300°F/Gas 2). Line thirty 30 ml (1 fl oz/⅛ cup) capacity mini-muffin holes with paper cases.

Combine the biscuits and butter in a bowl. Divide between the paper cases and refrigerate for 15 minutes.

Place the cream cheese and sugar in the bowl of an electric mixer and beat on medium–high speed for 2 minutes. Reduce the speed, add the egg and beat well, scraping down the sides of the bowl as required. Add the flour, and lemon juice and zest, and combine well.

Transfer the mixture to a large piping bag fitted with a 3 cm (1¼ inch) plain nozzle and pipe into the paper cases, filling them three-quarters full. Top each cheesecake with 2–3 blueberries, pushing them slightly into the mixture. Bake for 15 minutes or until set. Cool in the tins for 5 minutes, then turn out onto wire racks and cool for 30 minutes. Refrigerate for at least 3 hours.

Meanwhile, to make the blueberry sauce, place all of the ingredients in a saucepan over low heat and stir gently until the sugar has dissolved and the blueberries release some of their juices. Using a slotted spoon, remove the berries and set aside. Increase the heat to high and cook until the liquid has reduced by one-third. Pour over the berries, leave to cool completely, then refrigerate until chilled.

To serve, spoon 1 tablespoon of sauce over each cheesecake.

layered jellies with
citrus and pomegranate

seeds from 4 small
   pomegranates
Persian fairy floss

BLOOD ORANGE JELLY
500 ml (18 fl oz/2 cups)
   blood orange juice,
   strained
220 g (7¾ oz/1 cup)
   caster (superfine) sugar
1 tablespoon powdered
   gelatine

RUBY GRAPEFRUIT JELLY
1 litre (35 fl oz/4 cups)
   ruby grapefruit juice,
   strained
220 g (7¾ oz/1 cup)
   caster (superfine) sugar
2 tablespoons powdered
   gelatine

POMEGRANATE JELLY
500 ml (18 fl oz/2 cups)
   pomegranate juice,
   strained
165 g (5¾ oz/¾ cup)
   caster (superfine) sugar
1 tablespoon powdered
   gelatine

To make the blood orange jelly, place the juice and sugar in a small saucepan over medium heat and stir until the sugar has dissolved. Remove from the heat, add the gelatine and stir until dissolved. Cool slightly, then divide among sixteen 125 ml (4½ fl oz/½ cup) capacity jelly moulds and refrigerate for 1 hour or until set.

To make the ruby grapefruit jelly, place the juice and sugar in a small saucepan over medium heat and stir until the sugar has dissolved. Remove from the heat, add the gelatine and stir until dissolved. Cool slightly, then distribute evenly into each of the moulds and refrigerate for 1 hour or until set.

To make the pomegranate jelly, place the juice and sugar in a small saucepan over medium heat and stir until the sugar has dissolved. Remove from the heat, add the gelatine and stir until dissolved. Cool slightly, then distribute evenly into each of the moulds and refrigerate for 1 hour or until set.

To serve, unmould the jellies onto serving plates, scatter the pomegranate seeds around and garnish with the fairy floss.

profiteroles with
chocolate-espresso sauce

1 litre (35 fl oz/4 cups)
   coffee ice-cream

PROFITEROLES
125 g (4½ oz) unsalted
   butter
2 teaspoons caster
   (superfine) sugar
185 g (6½ oz/1¼ cups)
   plain (all-purpose) flour
4 eggs

CHOCOLATE-ESPRESSO
   SAUCE
150 g (5½ oz) dark
   chocolate (65% cocoa
   solids), finely chopped
55 g (2 oz/¼ cup) caster
   (superfine) sugar
20 g (¾ oz) unsalted
   butter
125 ml (4½ fl oz/½ cup)
   thickened cream
125 ml (4½ fl oz/½ cup)
   espresso coffee

To make the profiteroles, preheat the oven to 210°C
(415°F/Gas 6–7). Line 2 baking trays with baking paper.
Place the butter, sugar and 250 ml (9 fl oz/1 cup) water
in a saucepan over medium heat and bring to the boil.
Add the flour and stir vigorously with a wooden spoon
until the dough comes together to form a ball. Continue
stirring for 2–3 minutes, then remove from the heat.
Transfer to the bowl of an electric mixer fitted with a
paddle attachment. Add the eggs, one at a time, beating
well after each addition.

Transfer the warm dough to a large piping bag fitted
with a 1 cm (½ inch) plain nozzle and pipe 2.5–3 cm
(1–1¼ inch) rounds about 2.5 cm (1 inch) apart onto the
trays. Bake for 15 minutes, then reduce the heat to 180°C
(350°F/Gas 4) and bake for a further 7–10 minutes. To test
if the profiteroles are cooked, cut one in half; it should be
hollow and dry inside, not eggy. Cool completely on
wire racks.

To make the sauce, place all of the ingredients in the
top of a double boiler over medium heat and stir until the
chocolate has melted and the sugar has dissolved.
Remove from the heat and keep warm.

To serve, halve each profiterole. Using a small
ice-cream scoop, scoop out balls of ice-cream and place
on the profiterole bases. Sandwich with the tops and
drizzle with the sauce.

122

mint brownie
ice-cream sandwiches

makes 16

1 litre (35 fl oz/4 cups)
mint chocolate-chip
ice-cream

MINT BROWNIE
125 g (4½ oz) unsalted
butter
125 g (4½ oz) dark
chocolate (70% cocoa
solids), finely chopped
110 g (3¾ oz/½ cup) caster
(superfine) sugar
95 g (3⅓ oz/½ cup lightly
packed) soft
brown sugar
2 eggs
1½ teaspoons natural mint
extract
75 g (2¾ oz/½ cup) plain
(all-purpose) flour, sifted

To make the mint brownie, preheat the oven to 180°C (350°F/Gas 4). Grease and line two 18 cm x 18 cm (7 inch x 7 inch) cake tins with baking paper. Place the butter and chocolate in the top of a double boiler over medium heat and stir until melted and smooth. Remove from the heat and cool slightly.

Place the sugars, eggs and mint extract in the bowl of an electric mixer and beat on medium speed for 3–5 minutes until light and combined. Add the chocolate mixture and mix well, scraping down the sides of the bowl as required. Add the flour and beat until just combined. Divide between the tins and bake for 12–14 minutes until cooked but still fudgy, and a skewer inserted comes out with moist crumbs. Cool for 5 minutes in the tins, then remove and cool completely on wire racks.

Place the ice-cream in the refrigerator for 10 minutes or until slightly softened. Line an 18 cm x 18 cm (7 inch x 7 inch) cake tin with plastic wrap, overhanging each side by 10 cm (4 inches). Place one of the brownie slabs in the base, cover with the ice-cream in a thick layer and top with the remaining brownie slab. Cover with plastic wrap and freeze for 4–5 hours or overnight.

To serve, use the overhanging plastic wrap to lift out the brownie sandwich onto a chopping board and slice into 4 cm x 4 cm (1½ inch x 1½ inch) squares.

125

blood orange
macarons

120 g (4¼ oz) almond meal
   (ground almonds)
220 g (7¾ oz) icing
   (confectioners') sugar
110 g (3¾ oz) egg white
30 g (1 oz) caster
   (superfine) sugar
1 teaspoon natural
   orange extract
orange or red food
   colouring, paste or
   powdered is preferable

BLOOD ORANGE CURD
6 egg yolks
125 ml (4½ fl oz/½ cup)
   blood orange juice,
   strained
1½ tablespoons lemon
   juice
165 g (5¾ oz/¾ cup)
   caster (superfine) sugar
80 g (2¾ oz) unsalted
   butter, cubed

Line 2 baking trays with baking paper. Process the almond meal and icing sugar in a food processor until combined, then sift twice. Place the egg white in the bowl of an electric mixer and beat on medium speed until frothy, then increase the speed while gradually adding the caster sugar. Continue beating until stiff peaks form. Mix in the orange extract and colouring. Fold one-third into the almond mixture and combine well. Gently fold the remaining egg white mixture through; it should be glossy and thick, not thin and runny.

Transfer to a piping bag fitted with a 5 mm (¼ inch) plain nozzle and pipe 3 cm (1¼ inch) circles about 3 cm (1¼ inches) apart onto the trays. Leave at room temperature for 1–6 hours (depending on the humidity) until a crust forms; the macarons should be not sticky to the touch.

To make the curd, place the egg yolks, juices and sugar in a saucepan over medium–low heat and stir continuously for 8–9 minutes until thick and the mixture coats a wooden spoon. Remove from the heat and add the butter, 1 cube at a time, beating well after each addition. Cover with plastic wrap and refrigerate for 1 hour.

Preheat the oven to 140°C (275°F/Gas 1). Bake the macarons for 15–18 minutes until they rise slightly. Immediately slide the macarons and paper off the trays onto wire racks to cool completely.

Transfer the blood orange curd to a piping bag fitted with a 1 cm (½ inch) plain nozzle and pipe 1-teaspoon amounts onto half of the macarons. Sandwich with the remaining macarons.

choc-mint whoopie
pies with marshmallow frosting

makes 12

150 g (5½ oz/1 cup) plain
  (all-purpose) flour
60 g (2¼ oz/½ cup) cocoa
  powder
½ teaspoon bicarbonate
  of soda (baking soda)
145 g (5¼ oz/⅔ cup)
  caster (superfine) sugar
90 g (3¼ oz) unsalted
  butter, at room
  temperature
1 egg
½ teaspoon natural
  vanilla extract
1 teaspoon mint extract
250 ml (9 fl oz/1 cup) milk
120 g (4¼ oz) crushed
  peppermint candies
  for decoration

MARSHMALLOW
  FROSTING
3 egg whites
165 g (5¾ oz/¾ cup)
  caster (superfine) sugar
¼ teaspoon cream of
  tartar
2 teaspoons peppermint
  schnapps

Preheat the oven to 175°C (340°F/Gas 3–4). Grease and flour 2 baking trays or 3 whoopie pie tins. Sift the flour, cocoa and bicarbonate of soda together into a large bowl. Place the sugar and butter in the bowl of an electric mixer and beat on medium speed for 1–2 minutes until light and creamy. Add the egg and the vanilla and mint extracts and beat for a further minute. Reduce the speed and add the flour mixture in 3 batches, alternating with the milk, and beat until combined, scraping down the sides of the bowl as required.

Place 1½-tablespoon amounts of batter about 5 cm (2 inches) apart on the trays and bake for 8–10 minutes until cooked through. Cool for 5 minutes on the trays, then transfer to wire racks to cool completely.

Meanwhile, to make the marshmallow frosting, place the egg white, sugar and cream of tartar in the top of a double boiler over medium heat and whisk for 3 minutes or until warm and the sugar has dissolved. Remove from the heat, add the schnapps and, using electric beaters, beat for 6–7 minutes until glossy and stiff peaks form.

Transfer to a piping bag fitted with a 1 cm (½ inch) plain nozzle and pipe 2-tablespoon amounts of filling onto half of the cookies. Sandwich with the remaining cookies and roll the sides of the pies in the crushed peppermint candies to coat.

vanilla cheesecake
pops with ginger cookie crumbs

40 lollipop sticks
500 g (1 lb 2 oz) white
    chocolate, melted
125 g (4½ oz) gingersnap
    biscuits, crushed

VANILLA CHEESECAKE
750 g (1 lb 10 oz/3 cups)
    cream cheese, at room
    temperature
220 g (7¾ oz/1 cup)
    caster (superfine) sugar
3 eggs
1 egg yolk
185 g (6½ oz/¾ cup)
    sour cream
3 tablespoons plain
    (all-purpose) flour
1 vanilla bean, split and
    seeds scraped
45 g (1⅔ oz) candied
    ginger, thinly sliced

To make the cheesecake, preheat the oven to 160°C (315°F/Gas 2–3). Line a 22 cm (8½ inch) round cake tin with baking paper. Place the cream cheese and sugar in the bowl of an electric mixer and beat on medium speed for 1–2 minutes until smooth and combined. Add the eggs and egg yolk, one at a time, beating well after each addition. Add the sour cream, flour, vanilla seeds and ginger, and combine well. Pour into the tin and bake for 1¼ hours or until just set in the centre. Leave in the tin to cool completely, then refrigerate for 3–5 hours or overnight until chilled and very firm.

Line 2 baking trays with baking paper. Using a small ice-cream scoop, scoop balls of cheesecake onto the trays. Quickly roll each in the palms of your hands and shape into a neat ball. Insert a stick into each ball and freeze for 2 hours or until very firm.

Carefully dip each pop in the chocolate, gently twirling off any excess. Roll each pop in the crushed biscuit to coat well. Stand upright in a piece of polystyrene to set. Serve immediately or store in an airtight container in the refrigerator for 3–4 days.

ginger whoopie pies

with spiced candied-ginger cream

makes 15

260 g (9¼ oz/1¾ cups)
  plain (all-purpose) flour
1 teaspoon bicarbonate of
  soda (baking soda)
pinch of salt
1 teaspoon ground ginger
110 g (3¾ oz/½ cup) caster
  (superfine) sugar
95 g (3⅓ oz/½ cup lightly
  packed) brown sugar
125 g (4½ oz) unsalted
  butter, at room
  temperature
½ teaspoon natural vanilla
  extract
1 egg
250 ml (9 fl oz/1 cup) milk

SPICED CANDIED-
  GINGER CREAM
375 g (13 oz/1½ cups)
  cream cheese, at room
  temperature
75 g (2¾ oz) unsalted
  butter, at room
  temperature
2 teaspoons maple syrup
125 g (4½ oz/1 cup) icing
  (confectioners') sugar
1 teaspoon ground
  cinnamon
1 teaspoon ground nutmeg
35 g (1¼ oz) candied ginger,
  chopped

Preheat the oven to 175°C (340°F/Gas 3–4). Grease and flour 2 baking trays or 3 whoopie pie tins. Sift the flour, bicarbonate of soda, salt and ginger together into a large bowl. Place the sugars and butter in the bowl of an electric mixer and beat on medium speed for 1–2 minutes until light and creamy. Add the vanilla extract and egg and beat for a further minute. Reduce the speed and add the flour mixture in 3 batches, alternating with the milk, and beating until combined, scraping down the sides of the bowl as required.

Place 1½-tablespoon amounts of batter about 5 cm (2 inches) apart on the trays and bake for 8–10 minutes until cooked through. Cool for 5 minutes on the trays, then transfer to wire racks to cool completely.

Meanwhile, to make the ginger cream, place the cream cheese and butter in the bowl of an electric mixer and beat on medium speed for 2–3 minutes until combined and smooth. Reduce the speed and add the maple syrup, icing sugar and spices, and beat until combined. Fold in the candied ginger, cover with plastic wrap and refrigerate for 20 minutes or until firm.

Transfer to a piping bag fitted with a 1 cm (½ inch) plain nozzle and pipe 2-tablespoon amounts of filling onto half of the cookies. Sandwich with the remaining cookies.

133

watermelon
margarita pops with sweet and salty lime wedges

550 g (1 lb 4 oz) seedless watermelon, cut into small chunks
40 ml (1¼ fl oz) lime juice
40 ml (1¼ fl oz) agave syrup (see note)
45 ml (1⅔ fl oz) tequila
15 ml (½ fl oz) Cointreau
12 popsicle sticks
2 tablespoons fine sea salt
2 tablespoons caster (superfine) sugar
10 lime wedges

Combine the watermelon, lime juice, agave syrup, tequila and Cointreau in a bowl and leave for 20 minutes. Transfer to a blender and pulse until juicy but with chunks of watermelon remaining.

Pour into twelve 60 ml (2 fl oz/¼ cup) capacity popsicle moulds. Cover with plastic wrap and insert a stick through the plastic into each pop. Freeze for 8–10 hours until completely frozen.

To serve, place the salt and sugar on separate plates. Dip one side of each lime wedge in the salt, then the other side in the sugar. Skewer a lime wedge onto each popsicle stick.

Note: Agave syrup is available from health food shops.

banana daiquiri
cupcakes

makes 36

150 g (5½ oz/1 cup) plain
(all-purpose) flour
½ teaspoon bicarbonate
of soda (baking soda)
¼ teaspoon baking
powder
175 g (6 oz/about 2)
mashed banana
3 tablespoons buttermilk
30 ml (1 fl oz) dark rum
65 g (2¼ oz) unsalted
butter, at room
temperature
95 g (3⅓ oz/½ cup
lightly packed) soft
brown sugar
1 egg

COCONUT AND
RUM FROSTING
2 egg whites
110 g (3¾ oz/½ cup) caster
(superfine) sugar
3 tablespoons
glucose syrup
40 ml (1¼ fl oz) dark rum
1 teaspoon natural
coconut extract
30 g (1 oz/½ cup)
shredded coconut,
toasted (optional)

Preheat the oven to 180°C (350°F/Gas 4). Line thirty-six 30 ml (1 fl oz/⅛ cup) capacity mini-muffin holes with paper cases.

Sift the flour, bicarbonate of soda and baking powder together into a bowl. Combine the banana, buttermilk and rum. Place the butter and sugar in the bowl of an electric mixer and beat on medium speed for 2–3 minutes until light and creamy. Add the egg and beat well. Add the banana mixture in 3 batches, alternating with the flour mixture and beating until combined, scraping down the sides of the bowl as required.

Transfer the batter to a large piping bag fitted with a 1 cm (½ inch) plain nozzle and pipe into the cases, filling them three-quarters full. Bake for 10 minutes or until lightly golden and they spring back lightly to the touch. Cool in the tins for 1–2 minutes, then turn out onto wire racks to cool completely.

To make the frosting, place the egg white, sugar, glucose and 2 tablespoons water in the top of a double boiler over medium heat and, using electric beaters, beat for 7–8 minutes until glossy and stiff. Add the rum and coconut extract, and beat for a further minute. Immediately frost the cupcakes and top with the shredded coconut.

s'mores cupcakes

180 g (6⅓ oz) plain
(all-purpose) flour
1 teaspoon baking powder
30 g (1 oz/¼ cup) cocoa
powder
150 g (5½ oz) unsalted
butter
150 g (5½ oz) caster
(superfine) sugar
1 teaspoon natural vanilla
extract
3 eggs
3 tablespoons milk
50 g (1¾ oz/⅓ cup) mini
milk chocolate chips

COOKIE CRUMBS
2 wheat digestive biscuits,
finely crushed
¾ teaspoon caster
(superfine) sugar
¼ teaspoon ground
cinnamon

CHOCOLATE SAUCE
85 g (3 oz/½ cup) mini
milk chocolate chips
3 tablespoons pouring
(single) cream
1 teaspoon unsalted butter

Preheat the oven to 180°C (350°F/Gas 4). Line forty-two 30 ml (1 fl oz/⅛ cup) capacity mini-muffin holes with paper cases.

Sift the flour, baking powder and cocoa together into a bowl.

Place the butter, sugar and vanilla extract in the bowl of an electric mixer and beat on medium speed for 2–3 minutes until light and creamy. Add the eggs, one at a time, beating well after each addition and scraping down the sides of the bowl as required. Add the flour mixture in 2 batches, alternating with the milk. Add the chocolate chips and mix until just combined.

Transfer the batter to a large piping bag fitted with a 3 cm (1¼ inch) plain nozzle and pipe into the cases until three-quarters full.

Bake for 10 minutes or until just cooked and they spring back lightly to the touch. Cool for 1–2 minutes in the tins, then turn out onto wire racks to cool completely.

To make the cookie crumbs, place all of the ingredients in a bowl and combine well. Set aside.

To make the chocolate sauce, place the chocolate, cream and butter in the top of a double boiler over medium heat and stir until melted and smooth. Leave to cool slightly.

To make the frosting, place the egg white, sugar and cream of tartar in the top of a double boiler over medium heat and whisk for 3 minutes or until the sugar has dissolved and the mixture is warm. Remove from the heat, add the vanilla extract and, using electric beaters, beat for 6–7 minutes until stiff peaks form. Immediately transfer into a piping bag fitted with a 1 cm (½ inch) plain nozzle and pipe onto the cupcakes. Lightly toast the frosting with a kitchen blowtorch, then drizzle each cupcake with the sauce and sprinkle with the crumbs.

3 egg whites

165 g (5¾ oz/¾ cup)
  caster (superfine) sugar

¼ teaspoon cream of
  tartar

½ teaspoon natural vanilla
  extract

* meringue

130 g (4¾ oz) caster
(superfine) sugar
95 g (3⅓ oz) egg white
⅛ teaspoon salt

lemon meringue
cupcakes

185 g (6½ oz/1¼ cups)
plain (all-purpose) flour

1½ teaspoons baking
powder

125 g (4½ oz) unsalted
butter, at room
temperature

145 g (5¼ oz/⅔ cup)
caster (superfine) sugar

2 eggs

125 ml (4½ fl oz/½ cup)
milk

½ teaspoon natural
lemon extract

1 tablespoon finely grated
lemon zest

60 g (2¼ oz/¼ cup)
store-bought
lemon curd

Preheat the oven to 175°C (340°F/Gas 3–4). Line twelve 80 ml (2½ fl oz/⅓ cup) capacity muffin holes with paper cases. Sift the flour and baking powder together into a bowl. Place the butter and sugar in the bowl of an electric mixer and beat for 2–3 minutes until light and creamy. Add the eggs, one at a time, beating well after each addition. Add the flour mixture in 3 batches, alternating with the milk and beating until combined, scraping down the sides of the bowl as required. Add the lemon extract and zest, and beat to combine. Divide between the cases and bake for 18–20 minutes until lightly golden and a skewer inserted comes out clean. Cool in the tin for 4–5 minutes, then turn out onto wire racks to cool completely.

Using a melon baller, remove a scoop of cake from each cupcake. Fill each hole with 1–1½ tablespoons of lemon curd.

To make the meringue, place all of the ingredients in the top of a double boiler over medium heat and whisk continuously for 3–4 minutes until the mixture is hot to the touch and reaches 50°C (122°F) on a candy thermometer. Remove the bowl and, using electric beaters, beat the mixture on high speed until glossy and stiff peaks form. Immediately cover each cupcake with meringue using a spatula, then lightly toast with a kitchen blowtorch.

glitter pops

80 g (2¾ oz) unsalted
    butter, at room
    temperature
250 g (9 oz/1 cup) cream
    cheese, at room
    temperature
125 g (4½ oz/1 cup) icing
    (confectioners') sugar
2 tablespoons white
    chocolate liqueur
50 lollipop sticks
650 g (1 lb 7 oz) white
    chocolate, melted
75 g (2¾ oz/⅓ cup)
    gold sanding sugar
    (see note)

To make the white chocolate cake, preheat the oven to 180°C (350°F/Gas 4). Grease and line a 31 cm x 21 cm x 5 cm (12½ inch x 8¼ inch x 2 inch) cake tin with baking paper. Sift the flour, baking powder and salt together into a bowl. Place the butter and sugar in the bowl of an electric mixer and beat on medium speed for 2–3 minutes until light and creamy. Add the eggs, one at a time, beating well after each addition. Add the sour cream and liqueur and mix well. Add the milk and vinegar in 2 batches, alternating with the flour mixture and beating until combined, scraping down the sides of the bowl as required. Pour into the tin and bake for 35–40 minutes until a skewer inserted comes out clean. Cool completely in the tin. Slice off the sides, top and bottom of the cake and discard. Finely crumble the remaining cake into a large bowl.

Place the butter and cream cheese in the bowl of an electric mixer and beat on medium speed for 2 minutes or until smooth. Add the icing sugar and liqueur and mix well. Add to the crumbled cake and mix well; the mixture should stick together when squeezed in your hands.

Line 2 baking trays with baking paper and roll the mixture into 30 g (1 oz) balls. Insert a stick into each ball, place on the trays and refrigerate for 30 minutes or until chilled and firm.

Carefully dip each pop in the chocolate, gently twirling off any excess. Sprinkle with the sanding sugar and stand upright in a piece of polystyrene to set. Will keep in an airtight container in the refrigerator for 3–4 days.

Note: Sanding sugar is available from specialist cake decorating shops or online.

white chocolate cake

300 g (10½ oz/2 cups) plain
(all-purpose) flour
2 teaspoons baking powder
¼ teaspoon salt
225 g (8 oz) unsalted butter,
at room temperature
440 g (15½ oz/2 cups) caster
(superfine) sugar
4 eggs
85 g (3 oz/⅓ cup) sour cream
65 ml (2¼ fl oz) white
chocolate liqueur
65 ml (2¼ fl oz) milk
1 tablespoon white
vinegar

chocolate macarons
with espresso and cocoa nibs

Makes about 30

110 g (3¾ oz) almond meal
(ground almonds)
15 g (½ oz) cocoa powder
200 g (7 oz) icing
(confectioners') sugar
110 g (3¾ oz) egg white
30 g (1 oz) caster
(superfine) sugar

ESPRESSO GANACHE
80 ml (2½ fl oz/⅓ cup)
pouring (single) cream
2 teaspoons instant
coffee granules
120 g (4¼ oz) dark
chocolate (70% cocoa
solids), chopped
2 tablespoons cocoa nibs
(see note)

Line 2 baking trays with baking paper. Process the almond meal, cocoa and icing sugar in a food processor until combined, then sift twice. Place the egg white in the bowl of an electric mixer and beat on medium speed until frothy, then increase the speed while gradually adding the caster sugar. Continue beating until stiff peaks form. Fold one-third into the almond mixture and combine well. Gently fold the remaining egg white mixture through; it should be glossy and thick, not thin and runny.

Transfer to a piping bag fitted with a 5 mm (¼ inch) plain nozzle and pipe 3 cm (1¼ inch) circles about 3 cm (1¼ inches) apart onto the trays. Leave at room temperature for 1–6 hours (depending on the humidity) until a crust forms; the macarons should be not sticky to the touch.

Preheat the oven to 140°C (275°F/Gas 1). Bake the macarons for 15–18 minutes until they rise slightly. Immediately slide the macarons and paper off the trays onto wire racks to cool completely.

Meanwhile, to make the ganache, place the cream and the coffee granules in the top of a double boiler over medium heat and stir until the coffee has dissolved. Add the chocolate and stir until melted and smooth. Refrigerate for 20–25 minutes until firm but pliable, then gently stir the cocoa nibs through.

Transfer to a small piping bag fitted with a 1 cm (½ inch) plain nozzle and pipe 1-teaspoon amounts onto half of the macarons. Sandwich with the remaining macarons.

Note: Cocoa nibs are available from gourmet food shops.

145

brownie bites
with cheesecake topping

125 g (4½ oz) unsalted
   butter
200 g (7 oz) dark
   chocolate (70% cocoa
   solids), finely chopped
220 g (7¾ oz/1 cup)
   caster (superfine) sugar
3 eggs
150 g (5½ oz/1 cup) plain
   (all-purpose) flour
1 teaspoon natural
   vanilla extract
¼ teaspoon salt

CHEESECAKE TOPPING
180 g (6⅓ oz) cream
   cheese
75 g (2¾ oz/⅓ cup)
   caster (superfine) sugar
1 egg
1 tablespoon plain
   (all-purpose) flour
1 teaspoon natural
   vanilla extract

Preheat the oven to 165°C (320°F/Gas 3). Grease and line a 27 cm x 17.5 cm (10¾ inch x 6¾ inch) slice tin with baking paper.

To make the cheesecake topping, place the cream cheese and sugar in the bowl of an electric mixer and beat on medium speed for 2–3 minutes until smooth. Add the egg, flour and vanilla extract, and beat to combine. Transfer to a bowl and set aside.

Place the butter and chocolate in the top of a double boiler over medium heat and stir until melted and smooth. Place the sugar and eggs in the bowl of an electric mixer and beat for 2 minutes or until light and creamy. Add the flour, vanilla extract and salt, and beat to combine.

Pour the chocolate mixture into the tin. Spoon the topping over and spread evenly. Using a butter knife, cut into the mixture to create a marbled effect. Bake for 30–35 minutes until cooked through. Cool completely in the tin, then slice into 2.5 cm x 2.5 cm (1 inch x 1 inch) bites.

gingersnap and peach
ice-cream | sandwiches

makes 30

15 litres (52 fl oz/6 cups)
    peach ice-cream

GINGERSNAP COOKIES
300 g (10½ oz/2 cups)
    plain (all-purpose) flour
1½ teaspoons bicarbonate
    of soda (baking soda)
2 teaspoons ground
    cinnamon
1 teaspoon ground allspice
½ teaspoon salt
125 g (4½ oz) unsalted
    butter, at room
    temperature
220 g (7¾ oz/1 cup)
    golden caster
    (superfine) sugar
    (see note)
1 egg, lightly beaten
85 ml (4 fl oz/¼ cup)
    unsulphured blackstrap
    molasses (see note)
2 teaspoons freshly
    grated ginger
½ cup minced
    candied ginger
140 g (5 oz/⅔ cup) raw
    (demerara) sugar

To make the cookies, preheat the oven to 180°C (350°F/ Gas 4). Line 2 baking trays with baking paper. Sift the flour, bicarbonate of soda, spices and salt together into a bowl. Place the butter and caster sugar in the bowl of an electric mixer and beat on medium speed for 2–3 minutes until light and creamy. Add the egg and molasses and mix well. Add the flour mixture and gingers, and mix well, scraping down the sides of the bowl.

Roll the dough into 15 g (½ oz) balls. Roll each in the raw sugar, place 3–5 cm (1¼–2 inches) apart on the trays and flatten with the base of a glass dipped in raw sugar. Bake for 7–9 minutes until crisp. Cool completely on the trays. Use immediately or store in an airtight container for up to 4 days.

Line 2 baking trays with baking paper. Use a small ice-cream scoop or melon baller to scoop out 30 balls of ice-cream, place on the trays and refrigerate for 2–3 minutes until slightly softened. Place the balls on half of the cookies and sandwich with the remaining cookies. Place in the freezer until ready to serve.

Note: Golden caster sugar is available from gourmet food shops. Blackstrap molasses is available from health food shops. To make slightly larger ice-cream sandwiches, see note on page 154.

149

g & t pops

85 ml (2¾ fl oz) lemon
  juice
60 ml (2 fl oz/¼ cup)
  lime juice
165 g (5¾ oz/¾ cup)
  caster (superfine) sugar
10 small lime or
  lemon slices
300 ml (10½ fl oz) tonic
  water
65 ml (2¼ fl oz) gin
10 popsicle sticks

Place the lemon and lime juices, sugar and lime slices in a non-reactive saucepan over medium heat and simmer for 1–2 minutes until the sugar has dissolved. Remove from the heat and leave to cool for 5 minutes.

Add the tonic and gin to the syrup and stir to combine. Pour into ten 60 ml (2 fl oz/¼ cup) popsicle moulds and add a lime slice to each. Cover with plastic wrap and insert a stick through the plastic into each pop. Freeze for 8–10 hours until completely frozen.

lemon madeleines
with limoncello glaze

makes 48

130 g (4¾ oz) plain
  (all-purpose) flour
½ teaspoon baking
  powder
3 eggs
130 g (4¾ oz) caster
  (superfine) sugar
2 tablespoons finely
  grated lemon zest
1 teaspoon natural
  lemon extract
115 g (4 oz) unsalted
  butter, melted

LIMONCELLO GLAZE
190 g (6¾ oz/1½ cups)
  icing (confectioners')
  sugar
2 tablespoons lemon juice
40 ml (1¼ fl oz) limoncello

Preheat the oven to 180°C (350°F/Gas 4). Grease 2 madeleine tins.

Sift the flour and baking powder together into a bowl. Place the eggs, sugar, and lemon zest and extract in the bowl of an electric mixer and whisk on medium–high speed for 4–5 minutes until pale and thickened. Gently fold in the flour mixture. Fold in the butter, a little at a time, folding well after each addition. Leave to rest for 15–20 minutes.

Meanwhile, to make the glaze, whisk all of the ingredients in a bowl until combined and smooth. Set aside.

Fill the tins with the madeleine mixture until three-quarters full and bake for 7–9 minutes until the edges are light golden. Turn out onto wire racks and cool for 2–3 minutes, then spoon the glaze over to coat.

Repeat with the remaining batter. Madeleines are best eaten on the day of making.

153

chocolate indulgence
ice-cream sandwiches

1 litre (35 fl oz/4 cups)
   chocolate ice-cream

CHOCOLATE CHIP
   COOKIES
150 g (5½ oz/1 cup) plain
   (all-purpose) flour, plus
   2 tablespoons extra
1 teaspoon baking
   powder
40 g (1½ oz/⅓ cup)
   cocoa powder
125 g (4½ oz) unsalted
   butter, at room
   temperature
165 g (5¾ oz/¾ cup)
   caster (superfine) sugar
1 teaspoon natural
   vanilla extract
1 egg
120 g (4¼ oz/¾ cup) mini
   milk-chocolate chips
120 g (4¼ oz/¾ cup) mini
   dark-chocolate chips

To make the cookies, preheat the oven to 175°C (340°F/Gas 3–4). Line 2 baking trays with baking paper. Sift together the flour, baking powder and cocoa. Place the butter, sugar and vanilla extract in the bowl of an electric mixer and beat on medium speed for 1–2 minutes until light and creamy. Add the egg and mix well. Add the flour mixture and mix well. Stir in the chocolate chips.

Roll the dough into 20 g (¾ oz) balls and place on the trays 3–5 cm (1¼–2 inches) apart. Flatten each with the palm of your hand or the base of a floured glass. Bake for 7 minutes or until fragrant. Cool for 2 minutes on the trays, then remove to wire racks and cool completely. Use immediately or store in an airtight container for up to 4 days.

Line 2 baking trays with baking paper. Use a small ice-cream scoop or melon baller to scoop out 20 balls of ice-cream, place on the trays and refrigerate for 2–3 minutes until slightly softened. Place the balls on half of the cookies, then sandwich with the remaining cookies. Place on the trays and freeze until firm.

Note: To make slightly larger ice-cream sandwiches, roll the mixture into 25 g (1 oz) balls and bake for 8–9 minutes; makes 15 sandwiches. Alternatively, roll the mixture into 30 g (1 oz) balls and bake for 10–11 minutes; makes 13 sandwiches.

pimm's pops

makes 10

250 ml (9 fl oz/1 cup)
  ginger ale
250 ml (9 fl oz/1 cup)
  lemonade
185 ml (6 fl oz/¾ cup)
  Pimm's
8 mint leaves
2 orange slices
2 lemon slices
4 small cucumber slices
4 strawberries, halved
10 popsicle sticks

Place all the ingredients, except the popsicle sticks, in a large measuring jug and refrigerate for 1–2 hours to infuse.

Pour the Pimm's mixture into ten 60 ml (2 fl oz/¼ cup) capacity popsicle moulds and add a mint leaf, piece of fruit or slice of cucumber to each popsicle. Cover with plastic wrap and insert a stick through the plastic into each pop. Freeze for 8–10 hours until completely frozen.

black velvet

whoopie pies

225 g (8 oz/1½ cups) plain
   (all-purpose) flour
60 g (2¼ oz/½ cup) cocoa
   powder
1 teaspoon bicarbonate of
   soda (baking soda)
pinch of salt
160 g (5⅔ oz/1 cup)
   brown sugar
125 g (4½ oz) unsalted
   butter, at room
   temperature
1 teaspoon natural
   vanilla extract
1 egg
250 ml (9 fl oz/1 cup)
   buttermilk
½ teaspoon white vinegar

CREAM CHEESE
   FROSTING
375 g (13 oz/1½ cups)
   cream cheese, at
   room temperature
75 g (2¾ oz) unsalted
   butter, at room
   temperature
1 teaspoon natural
   vanilla extract
125 g (4½ oz/1 cup) icing
   (confectioners') sugar,
   sifted

Preheat the oven to 175°C (340°F/Gas 3–4). Grease and flour 2 baking trays or 3 whoopie pie tins. Sift the flour, cocoa, bicarbonate of soda and salt together into a large bowl. Place the sugar and butter in the bowl of an electric mixer and beat on medium speed for 1–2 minutes until light and creamy. Add the vanilla extract and egg, and beat for a further minute. Reduce the speed and add the flour mixture, in 3 batches, alternating with the buttermilk and beat until just combined, then beat in the vinegar, scraping down the sides of the bowl as required.

Place 1½-tablespoon amounts of batter about 5 cm (2 inches) apart on the trays and bake for 8–10 minutes until cooked through. Cool for 5 minutes on the trays, then transfer to wire racks to cool completely.

Meanwhile, to make the frosting, place the cream cheese, butter and vanilla extract in the bowl of an electric mixer and beat on medium–high speed for 2–3 minutes until combined and smooth. Reduce the speed, add the icing sugar and beat until combined. Cover with plastic wrap and refrigerate for 20–25 minutes until firm.

Transfer to a piping bag fitted with a 1 cm (½ inch) plain nozzle and pipe 2-tablespoon amounts of filling onto half of the cookies. Sandwich with the remaining cookies.

persian rose

macarons

Makes about 30

80 g (2¾ oz/¾ cup) almond meal (ground almonds)
40 g (1½ oz) pistachio kernels
220 g (7¾ oz) icing (confectioners') sugar
110 g (3¾ oz) egg white
30 g (1 oz) caster (superfine) sugar
green food colouring, paste or powdered is preferable

ROSE BUTTERCREAM
100 g (3½ oz) caster (superfine) sugar
2 egg whites
185 g (6½ oz) unsalted butter, cubed and at room temperature
3 teaspoons rosewater
pink food colouring, paste or powdered is preferable

Line 2 baking trays with baking paper. Process the almond meal, pistachios and icing sugar in a food processor until the pistachios are finely chopped, then sift twice. Place the egg white in the bowl of an electric mixer and beat on medium speed until frothy, then increase the speed while gradually adding the caster sugar. Beat until stiff peaks form. Mix in enough colouring for desired effect. Fold one-third into the almond mixture and combine well. Gently fold the remaining egg white mixture through; it should be glossy and thick, not thin and runny.

Transfer to a piping bag fitted with a 5 mm (¼ inch) plain nozzle and pipe 3 cm (1¼ inch) circles about 3 cm (1¼ inches) apart onto the trays. Leave at room temperature for 1–6 hours (depending on the humidity) until a crust forms; the macarons should be not sticky to the touch.

Preheat the oven to 140°C (275°F/Gas 1). Bake the macarons for 15–18 minutes until they rise slightly. Immediately slide the macarons and paper off the trays onto wire racks to cool completely.

To make the buttercream, place the sugar and egg white in the top of a double boiler over medium heat and whisk for 3–4 minutes until warm and the sugar has dissolved. Remove from the heat. Using electric beaters, beat the mixture on medium–high speed for 6–7 minutes until glossy and stiff peaks form. Reduce the speed and add the butter, 1 cube at a time, beating well after each addition. Mix in the rosewater and enough colouring for desired effect.

Transfer to a piping bag fitted with a 1 cm (½ inch) plain nozzle and pipe 1-teaspoon amounts onto half of the macarons. Sandwich with the remaining macarons.

161

double chocolate
whoopie pies

makes 12

150 g (5½ oz/1 cup) plain
(all-purpose) flour
60 g (2¼ oz/½ cup) cocoa
powder
½ teaspoon bicarbonate
of soda (baking soda)
145 g (5¼ oz/⅔ cup)
caster (superfine) sugar
90 g (3¼ oz) unsalted
butter, at room
temperature
1 teaspoon natural
vanilla extract
1 egg
250 ml (9 fl oz/1 cup) milk

CHOCOLATE
BUTTERCREAM
3 egg whites
145 g (5¼ oz/⅔ cup)
caster (superfine) sugar
160 g (5⅔ oz) unsalted
butter, cubed and at
room temperature
125 g (4½ oz) dark
chocolate (65% cocoa
solids), melted
2 tablespoons cocoa
powder

Preheat the oven to 175°C (340°F/Gas 3–4). Grease and flour 2 baking trays or 3 whoopie pie tins. Sift the flour, cocoa and bicarbonate of soda together into a large bowl. Place the sugar and butter in the bowl of an electric mixer and beat on medium speed for 2–3 minutes until light and creamy. Add the vanilla extract and egg, and beat for a further minute. Reduce the speed and add the flour mixture in 3 batches, alternating with the milk and beating until combined, scraping down the sides of the bowl as required.

Place 1½-tablespoon amounts of batter about 5 cm (2 inches) apart on the trays and bake for 8–10 minutes until cooked through. Cool for 5 minutes on the trays, then transfer to wire racks to cool completely.

Meanwhile, to make the chocolate buttercream, place the egg white and sugar in the top of a double boiler over medium heat and whisk for 3–4 minutes until warm and the sugar has dissolved. Remove from the heat. Using electric beaters, beat the mixture on medium–high speed for 6–7 minutes until glossy and stiff peaks form. Reduce the speed and add the butter, 1 cube at a time, beating well after each addition. Continue to beat for 2–3 minutes. Combine the melted chocolate and the cocoa. Add to the egg white mixture and beat to combine.

Transfer to a piping bag fitted with a 1 cm (½ inch) plain nozzle and pipe 2-tablespoon amounts of filling onto half of the cookies. Sandwich with the remaining cookies.

tangerine mimosa
jellies

makes 12

400 ml (14 fl oz) tangerine
    juice, strained
1.1 litres (38½ fl oz)
    sparkling white wine
400 g (14 oz) caster
    (superfine) sugar
2 tablespoons powdered
    gelatine
Persian fairy floss,
    to garnish

Place the juice, wine and sugar in a saucepan over medium–low heat and bring to a simmer, stirring until the sugar has dissolved. Remove from the heat.

Add the gelatine and stir until dissolved. Cool to room temperature, then pour into 12 champagne glasses and refrigerate for 2–3 hours until set.

To serve, garnish with the fairy floss.

peanut macarons
with salted caramel

80 g (2¾ oz/¾ cup)
   almond meal (ground
   almonds)
40 g (1½ oz) roasted
   peanuts
220 g (7¾ oz) icing
   (confectioners') sugar
110 g (3¾ oz) egg white
30 g (1 oz) caster
   (superfine) sugar

SALTED CARAMEL
   FILLING
110 g (3¾ oz/½ cup) caster
   (superfine) sugar
2 teaspoons glucose
   syrup
3 tablespoons pouring
   (single) cream
60 g (2¼ oz) butter, cubed
   and at room
   temperature
¼ teaspoon fleur de sel
   or fine sea salt flakes

Line 2 baking trays with baking paper. Process the almond meal, peanuts and icing sugar in a food processor until the peanuts are finely chopped, then sift twice. Place the egg white in the bowl of an electric mixer and beat on medium speed until frothy, then increase the speed while gradually adding the caster sugar. Beat until stiff peaks form. Fold one-third into the almond mixture and combine well. Gently fold through the remaining egg white mixture; it should be glossy and thick.

Transfer to a piping bag fitted with a 5 mm (¼ inch) plain nozzle and pipe 3 cm (1¼ inch) circles about 3 cm (1¼ inches) apart onto the trays. Leave at room temperature for 1–6 hours (depending on the humidity) until a crust forms; the macarons should be not sticky to the touch.

Preheat the oven to 140°C (275°F/Gas 1). Bake the macarons for 15–18 minutes until they rise slightly. Immediately slide the macarons and paper off the trays onto wire racks to cool completely.

To make the filling, place the sugar, glucose and 1½ tablespoons water in a saucepan over medium–high heat, swirling the pan (do not stir) to dissolve the sugar. Increase the heat to high, bring to the boil and cook until golden. Remove from the heat and carefully add the cream. Place over low heat, add the butter, 1 cube at a time, beating well after each addition. Mix in the salt. Leave to cool until thickened.

Transfer to a piping bag fitted with a 1 cm (½ inch) nozzle and pipe 1-teaspoon amounts onto half of the macarons. Sandwich with the remaining macarons.

meyer lemon
bars

makes 25

6 eggs
550 g (1 lb 4 oz/2½ cups)
  caster (superfine) sugar
75 g (2¾ oz/½ cup) plain
  (all-purpose) flour
250 ml (9 fl oz/1 cup)
  meyer lemon juice,
  strained (see note)
3 tablespoons finely
  grated meyer
  lemon zest

SWEET CRUST
225 g (8 oz/1½ cups) plain
  (all-purpose) flour
65 g (2⅓ oz/½ cup) icing
  (confectioners') sugar,
  plus extra for dusting
180 g (6⅓ oz) unsalted
  butter, cut into 10 pieces

Preheat the oven to 180°C (350°F/Gas 4).

To make the sweet crust, place the flour and sugar in the bowl of a food processor and pulse to combine. Add the butter, 1 piece at a time, until the mixture resembles pea-sized crumbs.

Press the mixture into the base of a 23.5 cm x 33.5 cm (9¼ inch x 13¼ inch) slice tin. Bake for 18–20 minutes until golden. Cool in the tin for 20–30 minutes.

Reduce the oven temperature to 150°C (300°F/Gas 2). Whisk the eggs, sugar, flour and lemon juice together in a bowl until combined and smooth. Stir in the zest and pour the mixture over the crust. Bake for 25–30 minutes until set. Remove from the oven and cool completely on a wire rack. Dust with icing sugar and cut into 6 cm x 2.5 cm (2½ inch x 1 inch) bars.

Note: Meyer lemons are available in the cooler months from select greengrocers and farmers' markets.

walnut brownie
pops

40 lollipop sticks
500 g (1 lb 2 oz) dark
  chocolate (70% cocoa
  solids), melted
chocolate sprinkles,
  for coating

WALNUT BROWNIE
300 g (10½ oz) dark
  chocolate (70% cocoa
  solids), finely chopped
185 g (6½ oz) unsalted
  butter, at room
  temperature
330 g (11¾ oz/1½ cups)
  caster (superfine) sugar
45 g (1¾ oz/¼ cup lightly
  packed) soft brown
  sugar
4 eggs, lightly beaten
2 teaspoons natural
  vanilla extract
150 g (5½ oz/1 cup) plain
  (all-purpose) flour
2 tablespoons cocoa
  powder
100 g (3½ oz/1 cup)
  walnuts, finely chopped

To make the walnut brownie, preheat the oven to 175°C (340°F/Gas 3–4). Grease and line a 31 cm x 21 cm x 5 cm (12½ inch x 8¼ inch x 2 inch) cake tin with baking paper. Place the chocolate and butter in the top of a double boiler over medium heat and stir until melted and smooth. Add the sugars and stir until dissolved. Remove from the heat and cool slightly. Add the egg and vanilla extract and stir to combine. Sift the flour and cocoa together into a large bowl, add the chocolate mixture, combine well and stir in the walnuts.

Pour into the tin and bake for 25–30 minutes until cooked but still fudgy and a skewer inserted comes out with moist crumbs. Cool completely in the tin.

Line 2 baking trays with baking paper. Using a small ice-cream scoop, scoop out balls of brownie onto the trays. Quickly roll each in the palms of your hands to shape into a neat ball. Insert a stick into each ball and refrigerate for 2 hours or until well chilled and firm.

Carefully dip each pop in the melted chocolate, gently twirling off any excess. Roll each pop in the sprinkles to coat well. Stand upright in a piece of polystyrene to set. Serve immediately or store in an airtight container in the refrigerator for 3–4 days.

passionfruit
macarons

Makes about 30

120 g (4¼ oz) almond
   meal (ground almonds)
220 g (7¾ oz) icing
   (confectioners') sugar
110 g (3¾ oz) egg white
30 g (1 oz) caster
   (superfine) sugar
yellow food colouring,
   paste or powdered is
   preferable

PASSIONFRUIT CURD
5 egg yolks
165 g (5¾ oz/¾ cup)
   caster (superfine) sugar
125 ml (4½ fl oz/½ cup)
   passionfruit pulp
1 tablespoon lemon juice
80 g (2¾ oz) unsalted
   butter, cubed

Line 2 baking trays with baking paper. Process the almond meal and icing sugar in a food processor until combined, then sift twice. Place the egg white in the bowl of an electric mixer and beat on medium speed until frothy, then increase the speed while gradually adding the caster sugar. Continue beating until stiff peaks form. Mix in enough colouring for desired effect. Fold one-third into the almond mixture and combine well. Gently fold the remaining egg white mixture through; it should be glossy and thick, not thin and runny.

Transfer to a piping bag fitted with a 5 mm (¼ inch) plain nozzle and pipe 3 cm (1¼ inch) circles about 3 cm (1¼ inches) apart onto the trays. Leave at room temperature for 1–6 hours (depending on the humidity) until a crust forms; the macarons should be not sticky to the touch.

To make the passionfruit curd, place the egg yolks, sugar, passionfruit pulp and lemon juice in a saucepan over medium–low heat and, using a wooden spoon, stir continuously for 8–9 minutes until thick and the mixture coats the spoon. Remove from the heat and add the butter, 1 cube at a time, beating well after each addition. Cover with plastic wrap and refrigerate for 1 hour.

Preheat the oven to 140°C (275°F/Gas 1). Bake the macarons for 15–18 minutes until they rise slightly. Immediately slide the macarons and paper off the trays onto wire racks to cool completely.

Transfer the passionfruit curd to a piping bag fitted with a 1 cm (½ inch) plain nozzle and pipe 1-teaspoon amounts onto half of the macarons. Sandwich with the remaining macarons.

173

blueberry mojito
popsicles

makes 12

110 g (3¾ oz/½ cup)
golden caster
(superfine) sugar
¼ cup chopped mint
115 g (4 oz/¾ cup) fresh
blueberries
3 tablespoons lime juice
75 ml (2⅓ fl oz) rum
300 ml (10½ fl oz) soda
water
12 popsicle sticks

Place the sugar, mint, blueberries, lime juice and 3 tablespoons water in a saucepan over medium heat and simmer for 1–2 minutes until the sugar has dissolved. Remove from the heat and leave to cool for 5 minutes to infuse.

Add the rum and soda to the blueberry syrup and stir to combine. Pour into twelve 60 ml (2 fl oz/¼ cup) capacity popsicle moulds. Cover with plastic wrap and insert a stick through the plastic into each pop. Freeze for 8–10 hours until completely frozen.

*chocolate cake

- 110 g (3¾ oz) self-raising (self-rising) flour
- 40 g (1½ oz/⅓ cup) cocoa powder
- 200 g (7 oz) caster (superfine) sugar
- 80 g (2¾ oz) unsalted butter, at room temperature
- 125 g (4½ oz) dark chocolate (65% cocoa solids), finely chopped
- 2 eggs, lightly beaten
- 1 teaspoon natural vanilla extract

ice-cream
cake pops

makes 30

80 g (2¾ oz) unsalted
butter, at room
temperature
125 g (4½ oz/1 cup) icing
(confectioners') sugar
2 tablespoons cocoa
powder
2 tablespoons pouring
(single) cream
500 g (1 lb 2 oz) dark
chocolate (65% cocoa
solids), finely chopped
30 mini waffle ice-cream
cones
500 g (1 lb 2 oz) dark
chocolate (65% cocoa
solids), melted
200 g (7 oz) white
chocolate, melted
sprinkles, to decorate

To make the chocolate cake, preheat the oven to 180°C
(350°F/Gas 4). Grease and line a 22 cm (8½ inch) round
cake tin with baking paper. Sift the flour and cocoa
together into a large bowl. Combine the sugar and 125 ml
(4½ fl oz/½ cup) boiling water in the top of a double boiler
over medium heat and stir until dissolved. Add the butter
and chopped chocolate and stir until melted and smooth.
Cool slightly. Combine the egg and vanilla extract, add to
the flour mixture and mix well. Add the chocolate mixture
and mix well. Pour into the tin and bake for 30–35 minutes
until a skewer inserted comes out clean. Remove from
the tin and cool completely on a wire rack. Finely crumble
the cake into a large bowl.

Place the butter, icing sugar and cocoa in the bowl of
an electric mixer and beat for 1–2 minutes until light and
creamy. Add the cream and mix well. Add to the
crumbled cake and, using your hands, mix well; the
mixture should stick together when squeezed.

Line 2 baking trays with baking paper. Roll the mixture
into 30 g (1 oz) balls. Press each onto an ice-cream cone
and freeze for 15 minutes or until firm.

Carefully dip each pop in the melted dark chocolate,
gently twirling off any excess. Stand upright in a piece of
polystyrene to set. Using a teaspoon, drip some white
chocolate over the dark chocolate and coat with the
sprinkles. Serve immediately or store in an airtight
container in the refrigerator for 3–4 days.

makes 20

persian
florentines

35 g (1¼ oz) chopped
  candied orange peel
100 g (3½ oz) dried sour
  cherries
80 g (2¾ oz) flaked
  almonds
65 g (2⅓ oz) pistachio
  kernels, chopped
1¼ teaspoons orange
  blossom water
35 g (1¼ oz/¼ cup) plain
  (all-purpose) flour
40 g (1½ oz) unsalted
  butter
60 g (2¼ oz) caster
  (superfine) sugar
60 g (2¼ oz) honey
80 ml (2½ fl oz/⅓ cup)
  pouring (single) cream
85 g (3 oz) dark chocolate
  (70% cocoa solids),
  melted

Preheat the oven to 175°C (340°F/Gas 3–4). Line
2 baking trays with baking paper.

Place the orange peel, cherries, nuts, orange
blossom water and flour in a bowl and stir to combine.

Place the butter, sugar, honey and cream in a
saucepan over medium heat, bring to the boil and cook
until it reaches 112°C (234°F; soft-ball stage) on a candy
thermometer. Add to the fruit and nut mixture and stir
to combine.

Drop single tablespoon amounts of mixture about 5 cm
(2 inches) apart on the trays and flatten slightly. Bake for
12–14 minutes until golden and set. Allow to cool completely
on the trays.

Place the melted chocolate in a small piping bag fitted
with a 5 mm (¼ inch) plain nozzle and pipe stripes across
each cookie. Leave to set. Store in an airtight container for
up to 1 week.

strawberry tartlets
with sticky balsamic glaze

Makes about 50

300 g (10½ oz) goat's curd
200 g (7 oz) ricotta
3 teaspoons orange
blossom honey
1 teaspoon finely grated
orange zest
25 strawberries, halved

VANILLA SHORTCRUST
PASTRY
125 g (4½ oz) unsalted
butter, at room
temperature
80 g (2¾ oz) icing
(confectioners') sugar
1 egg yolk
½ vanilla bean, split and
seeds scraped
200 g (7 oz/1¼ cups) plain
(all-purpose) flour, sifted

BALSAMIC GLAZE
125 ml (4½ fl oz/½ cup)
good-quality balsamic
vinegar
115 g (4 oz/⅓ cup) honey

To make the pastry, place the butter and icing sugar in the bowl of an electric mixer and beat for 2–3 minutes until light and creamy. Add the egg yolk and vanilla seeds and beat to combine well. Add the flour and beat until just combined. Turn the dough out onto a floured surface, shape into a disc, wrap in plastic wrap and refrigerate for 1–2 hours.

Preheat the oven to 180°C (350°F/Gas 4).

Meanwhile, to make the balsamic glaze, place the vinegar and honey in a saucepan over medium heat and simmer until reduced by one-third and the mixture is thick and syrupy. Cool completely.

Roll the pastry dough into fifty 8 g (¼ oz) balls. Place each ball in a 3.5 cm (1¼ inch) fluted tartlet tin and press the pastry into the base and sides. Freeze for 10 minutes.

Place the pastry cases on baking trays and bake for 7–9 minutes until golden and cooked. If the pastry puffs up, use a teaspoon to gently push it down. Cool in the tins for 8–10 minutes, then turn out onto wire racks and cool completely.

To serve, combine the goat's curd, ricotta, honey and orange zest in a bowl. Transfer to a large piping bag fitted with a 5 mm (¼ inch) plain nozzle and pipe the mixture into the cases. Top each with a strawberry half and drizzle with the glaze.

hibiscus vodka
pops

12 g (½ oz/¼ cup) dried
   hibiscus flowers or
   3 hibiscus tea bags
   (see note)
60 ml (2 fl oz/¼ cup)
   agave syrup (see note)
60 ml (2 fl oz/¼ cup)
   vodka
10 popsicle sticks

Place the hibiscus flowers or tea bags in a heatproof jug, add 500 ml (18 fl oz/2 cups) boiling water and leave for 15 minutes to infuse.

Remove and discard the flowers or tea bags, add the agave syrup and stir until dissolved. Add the vodka and leave to cool slightly.

Pour into ten 60 ml (2 fl oz/¼ cup) capacity popsicle moulds. Cover with plastic wrap and insert a stick through the plastic into each pop. Freeze for 8–10 hours until completely frozen.

182

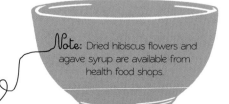

Note: Dried hibiscus flowers and agave syrup are available from health food shops.

chocolate tarts
with raspberry

Makes about 50

400 g (14 oz) dark
chocolate (65% cocoa
solids), finely chopped
550 ml (19 fl oz) thickened
cream
2 tablespoons natural
raspberry extract
(optional)
50 fresh raspberries

CHOCOLATE SHORTCRUST
PASTRY
175 g (6 oz) plain
(all-purpose) flour
25 g (1 oz) cocoa powder
125 g (4½ oz) unsalted
butter, at room
temperature
80 g (2¾ oz) icing
(confectioners') sugar
1 egg yolk

Place the chocolate and cream in the top of a double boiler over medium heat and stir until melted and smooth. Mix in the raspberry extract, if using. Transfer to a bowl and refrigerate for 20 minutes. Remove and stir, then refrigerate for a further 20 minutes. Repeat the process twice more and continue chilling for 4 hours or overnight.

Meanwhile, to make the pastry, sift the flour and cocoa together into a bowl. Place the butter and icing sugar in the bowl of an electric mixer and beat for 1–2 minutes until light and creamy. Add the egg yolk and combine well. Add the flour mixture and beat until just combined. Shape into a disc, wrap in plastic wrap and refrigerate for 1–2 hours.

Preheat the oven to 180°C (350°F/Gas 4).

Roll the pastry dough into fifty 8 g (¼ oz) balls. Place each ball in a 3.5 cm (1¼ inch) fluted tartlet tin and press the pastry into the base and sides. Freeze for 10 minutes.

Place the pastry cases on baking trays and bake for 7–9 minutes until golden and cooked. If the pastry puffs up, use a teaspoon to gently push it down. Cool in the tins for 8–10 minutes, then turn out onto wire racks to cool completely.

Transfer the chocolate mixture to the bowl of an electric mixer and beat on medium speed for 1–2 minutes until soft peaks form. Transfer to a large piping bag fitted with a 5 mm (¼ inch) plain nozzle and pipe into the cases. Top each tart with a raspberry.

vanilla whoopie
pies with white chocolate chips

260 g (9¼ oz/1¾ cups)
    plain (all-purpose) flour
1 teaspoon bicarbonate of
    soda (baking soda)
pinch of salt
110 g (3¾ oz/½ cup)
    caster (superfine) sugar
95 g (3⅓ oz/½ cup lightly
    packed) soft
    brown sugar
125 g (4½ oz) unsalted
    butter
1 vanilla bean, split and
    seeds scraped
1 egg
250 ml (9 fl oz/1 cup) milk
170 g (6 oz/1 cup) mini
    white chocolate chips,
    for decoration

Preheat the oven to 175°C (340°F/Gas 3–4). Grease and flour 2 baking trays or 3 whoopie pie tins. Sift the flour, bicarbonate of soda and salt together into a large bowl. Place the sugar and butter in the bowl of an electric mixer and beat on medium speed for 1–2 minutes until light and creamy. Add the vanilla seeds and egg, and beat for a further minute. Reduce the speed and add the flour mixture in 3 batches, alternating with the milk and beating until combined, scraping down the sides of the bowl as required.

Place 1½-tablespoon amounts of batter about 5 cm (2 inches) apart on the trays and bake for 8–10 minutes until cooked through. Cool for 5 minutes on the trays, then transfer to wire racks to cool completely.

Meanwhile to make the buttercream, place the egg white and sugar in the top of a double boiler over medium heat and whisk for 3–4 minutes until warm and the sugar has dissolved. Remove from the heat. Using electric beaters, beat the mixture on medium–high speed for 6–7 minutes until glossy and stiff peaks form. Reduce the speed and add the butter, 1 cube at a time, beating well after each addition. Continue to beat for 2–3 minutes. Add the vanilla seeds and beat to combine.

Transfer to a piping bag fitted with a 1 cm (½ inch) plain nozzle and pipe 2-tablespoon amounts of filling onto half of the cookies. Sandwich with the remaining cookies and roll the sides of the pies in the chocolate chips to coat.

3 egg whites
145 g (5¼ oz/⅔ cup)
    caster (superfine) sugar
160 g (5⅔ oz) unsalted
    butter, cubed and at
    room temperature
1 vanilla bean, split and
    seeds scraped

almond
corkscrews

makes 36

60 g (2¼ oz) unsalted
butter, at room
temperature
90 g (3¼ oz) caster
(superfine) sugar
2 egg whites, lightly
beaten, at room
temperature
1 teaspoon natural
almond extract
50 g (1¾ oz/⅓ cup) plain
(all-purpose) flour
65 g (2⅓ oz/¾ cup)
toasted flaked almonds

Preheat the oven to 180°C (350°F/Gas 4). Line 2 baking trays with baking paper.

Place the butter and sugar in the bowl of an electric mixer and beat on medium speed for 2–3 minutes until light and fluffy. Gradually add the egg white and almond extract and beat well until combined. Add the flour and beat to combine.

Transfer to a large piping bag fitted with a 5 mm (¼ inch) plain nozzle. Pipe six 7–8 cm (2¾–3¼ inch) long lines about 5 cm (2 inches) apart onto one tray. Only prepare one tray of cookies to bake at a time. Scatter the lines with one-third of the almonds and bake for 4–5 minutes until the edges begin to turn golden.

Remove from the oven. Working quickly, lift a cookie off the tray, using a spatula, then wrap it around the handle of a wooden spoon and leave to cool. Repeat with the remaining cookies. If the cookies cool and harden before being shaped, warm in the oven for 1 minute to soften. Slide the cooled corkscrews off the spoons.

Repeat the process with the remaining mixture, piping lines onto a cool baking tray each time. Store the corkscrews in an airtight container for up to 4 days.

189

black cherry
and kirsch jellies

1 litre (35 fl oz/4 cups)
   cherry juice
130 ml (4¼ fl oz) kirsch
   (cherry liqueur)
200 g (7 oz) caster
   (superfine) sugar
1½ tablespoons
   powdered gelatine
20 cherries, pitted
   and halved
dried miniature roses,
   to decorate

Place the cherry juice, kirsch and sugar in a saucepan over medium heat and bring to a simmer, stirring until the sugar has dissolved. Remove from the heat.

Add the gelatine and stir until dissolved. Cool to room temperature, then divide the liquid among twelve 100 ml (3½ fl oz) capacity jelly moulds. Divide the cherries among the moulds and refrigerate for 2–3 hours until set.

To serve, turn out and decorate with the roses.

jelly appletinis

makes 12

1 litre (35 fl oz/4 cups)
  apple juice
120 ml (4 fl oz) vodka
15 ml (½ fl oz) apple
  schnapps
200 g (7 oz) caster
  (superfine) sugar
1½ tablespoons
  powdered gelatine
apple slices, for garnish

Place the juice, vodka, schnapps and sugar in a saucepan over medium heat and bring to a simmer, stirring until the sugar has dissolved. Remove from the heat.

Add the gelatine and stir until dissolved. Cool to room temperature, then divide among twelve 100 ml (3½ fl oz) capacity jelly moulds. Refrigerate for 2–3 hours until set.

Garnish with apple slices to serve.

churros with
chilli-chocolate sauce

vegetable oil, for
deep-frying
125 g (4½ oz) unsalted
butter
¼ teaspoon salt
150 g (5½ oz/1 cup) plain
(all-purpose) flour
2 eggs
145 g (5¼ oz/⅔ cup)
caster (superfine) sugar
1½ teaspoons ground
cinnamon

CHOCOLATE-CHILLI
SAUCE
150 ml (5 fl oz) pouring
(single) cream
150 g (5½ oz) dark
chocolate chips
(65% cocoa solids)
1 teaspoon natural vanilla
extract
½ teaspoon ancho chilli
powder (see note)
½ teaspoon ground
cinnamon

Heat the oil in a deep-fryer or wide, heavy-based frying pan to 175°C (340°F).

Place the butter, salt and 250 ml (9 fl oz/1 cup) water in a saucepan over medium heat and bring to the boil. Add the flour and stir vigorously with a wooden spoon until the dough comes together to form a ball. Remove from the heat and add the eggs, beating well to combine; the dough should be shiny and soft.

Transfer to a large piping bag fitted with a small star nozzle. Carefully hold the piping bag over the oil with one hand and a small knife in the other. Pipe the dough into the oil and use the knife to slice off 7 cm (2¾ inch) lengths. Deep-fry 10–12 churros at a time for 2–3 minutes until golden and crisp. Drain on kitchen paper and keep warm. Repeat with the remaining dough.

To make the sauce, place the cream and chocolate in the top of a double boiler over medium heat and stir until melted and smooth. Add the vanilla extract, chilli powder and cinnamon and stir to combine. Remove from the heat and keep warm.

Combine the sugar and cinnamon in a shallow bowl and roll the churros in the mixture to coat. Serve with the sauce for dipping.

Note: Ancho chilli powder is available from gourmet food shops and delicatessens.

*pecan mascarpone

250 ml (9 fl oz/1 cup) pouring
  (single) cream
300 g (10½ oz) marscarpone,
  at room temperature
1 teaspoon natural vanilla
  extract
125 g (4½ oz/1 cup) icing
  (confectioners') sugar, sifted
½ teaspoon ground nutmeg
35 g (1¼ oz/⅓ cup) roasted
  pecans, chopped

spiced pumpkin
whoopie pies
with pecan mascarpone

150 g (5½ oz/1 cup) plain (all-purpose) flour
1 teaspoon ground cinnamon
½ teaspoon ground nutmeg
¼ teaspoon ground cloves
½ teaspoon bicarbonate of soda (baking soda)
½ teaspoon baking powder
185 g (6½ oz/1 cup lightly packed) soft brown sugar
125 g (4½ oz) unsalted butter, at room temperature
1 egg
250 g (9 oz/1 cup) pumpkin purée (see note)
½ teaspoon natural vanilla extract
125 ml (4½ fl oz/½ cup) milk

Preheat the oven to 175°C (340°F/Gas 3–4). Grease and flour 2 baking trays or 3 whoopie pie tins. Sift the flour, spices, bicarbonate of soda and baking powder together into a large bowl. Place the sugar and butter in the bowl of an electric mixer and beat on medium speed for 1–2 minutes until light and creamy. Add the egg, pumpkin and vanilla extract, and beat to combine well. Reduce the speed and add the flour mixture in 3 batches, alternating with the milk and beating until combined, scraping down the sides of the bowl as required.

Place 1½-tablespoon amounts of batter about 5 cm (2 inches) apart on the trays and bake for 9–12 minutes until cooked through. Cool for 5 minutes on the trays, then transfer to wire racks to cool completely.

To make the pecan mascarpone, whisk the cream until soft peaks form. Place the mascarpone and vanilla extract in the bowl of an electric mixer and beat on medium speed for 1–2 minutes until combined and smooth. Reduce the speed, add the icing sugar and nutmeg, and beat until combined. Fold in the whipped cream and the pecans. Cover with plastic wrap and refrigerate for 20 minutes or until firm.

Transfer to a piping bag fitted with a 1 cm (½ inch) plain nozzle and pipe 2-tablespoon amounts of filling onto half of the cookies. Sandwich with the remaining cookies.

Note: To make pumpkin purée, roast the pumpkin in a preheated 200°C (400°F/Gas 6) oven until tender, then process in a food processor until it becomes a smooth purée. Cool.

197

pecan caramel
tartlets

60 g (2¼ oz) unsalted
  butter
90 g (3¼ oz/¼ cup) dark
  corn syrup (see note)
1 tablespoon honey
65 g (2⅓ oz/½ cup) icing
  (confectioners') sugar
50 g (1¾ oz/½ cup)
  pecans, finely chopped
½ teaspoon natural
  vanilla extract

CREAM CHEESE PASTRY
125 g (4½ oz) butter, at
  room temperature
90 g (3¼ oz/⅓ cup) cup
  cream cheese, at room
  temperature
150 g (5½ oz/1 cup) plain
  (all-purpose) flour
30 g (1 oz/¼ cup) icing
  (confectioners') sugar
¼ teaspoon salt

Preheat the oven to 180°C (350°F/Gas 4). Grease twenty-four 30 ml (1 fl oz/⅛ cup) capacity mini-muffin holes.

To make the pastry, place the butter and cream cheese in the bowl of an electric mixer and beat on medium speed for 1–2 minutes until combined. Add the flour, icing sugar and salt, and beat to combine. Divide the pastry into 24 balls and place one in each muffin hole. Cover and refrigerate for 15–20 minutes.

Press the pastry into the base and sides of each hole. Cover and refrigerate until required.

Place the butter, corn syrup, honey and icing sugar in a saucepan over medium heat, bring to the boil and cook for 1 minute. Remove from the heat, add the pecans and vanilla extract and stir to combine. Spoon into the pastry cases and bake for 20–25 minutes until set. Cool in the tins for 10 minutes, then remove and cool completely on wire racks.

Note: Dark corn syrup is available from speciality grocery shops.

hazelnut macarons
with chocolate and frangelico

Makes about 30

60 g (2¼ oz) hazelnut meal
(ground hazelnut), plus
extra for sprinkling
60 g (2¼ oz) almond meal
(ground almonds)
220 g (7¾ oz) icing
(confectioners') sugar
110 g (3¾ oz) egg white
30 g (1 oz) caster
(superfine) sugar

CHOCOLATE AND
FRANGELICO GANACHE
110 g (3¾ oz) milk
chocolate, chopped
3 tablespoons pouring
(single) cream
50 ml (1¾ fl oz) Frangelico
or other hazelnut liqueur

Line 2 baking trays with baking paper. Process the hazelnut and almond meal, and icing sugar in a food processor until combined, then sift twice. Place the egg white in the bowl of an electric mixer and beat on medium speed until frothy, then increase the speed while gradually adding the caster sugar. Continue beating until stiff peaks form. Fold one-third into the hazelnut and almond mixture and combine well. Gently fold the remaining egg white mixture through; it should be glossy and thick, not thin and runny.

Transfer to a piping bag fitted with a 5 mm (¼ inch) plain nozzle and pipe 3 cm (1¼ inch) circles about 3 cm (1¼ inches) apart onto the trays. Leave at room temperature for 1–6 hours (depending on the humidity) until a crust forms; the macarons should be not sticky to the touch.

Preheat the oven to 140°C (275°F/Gas 1). Bake the macarons for 15–18 minutes until they rise slightly. Immediately slide the macarons and paper off the trays onto wire racks to cool completely.

Meanwhile, to make the chocolate and Frangelico ganache, place all of the ingredients in the top of a double boiler over medium heat and stir until melted and smooth. Refrigerate for 20–25 minutes until firm but pliable.

Transfer to a small piping bag fitted with a 1 cm (½ inch) plain nozzle and pipe 1-teaspoon amounts onto half of the macarons. Sandwich with the remaining macarons.

201

glazed vanilla
doughnuts and doughnut holes

250 g (9 oz/1⅔ cups) plain
    (all-purpose) flour
3 tablespoons caster
    (superfine) sugar
1 x 7 g (¼ oz) sachet
    dried yeast
½ teaspoon salt
80 ml (2½ fl oz/⅓ cup)
    milk
25 g (1 oz) unsalted
    butter
1 egg
vegetable oil, for
    deep-frying
sprinkles or icing
    (confectioners') sugar,
    for decoration

GLAZE
125 g (4½ oz/1 cup) icing
    (confectioners') sugar
1½–2 teaspoons milk
½ teaspoon natural
    vanilla extract

Line 2 baking trays with baking paper. Place 100 g (3½ oz) of the flour with the sugar, yeast and salt in the bowl of an electric mixer and stir to combine. Combine the milk and butter in a saucepan over medium heat and stir until melted. Pour the warmed milk into the flour mixture and beat on medium speed to combine. Add the egg and beat for 2–3 minutes. Add the remaining flour and beat to combine well. Knead the dough on a floured surface for 3–4 minutes until smooth. Place in a large oiled bowl, cover with plastic wrap and leave in a warm place for 1 hour or until doubled in size.

Roll out the dough on a floured surface to 5 mm (¼ inch) thick and, using a 5.5 cm (2¼ inch) round cutter, cut out circles. Use a 1 cm (½ inch) round cutter to cut out holes from the centre. Place the rings and holes on the trays. Re-roll the scraps and repeat. Cover and leave in a warm place for 35–40 minutes until doubled in size.

Heat the oil in a deep-fryer or wide, heavy-based frying pan over medium heat to 175°C (340°F). Deep-fry doughnuts in batches, turning often, until golden. Drain on kitchen paper, then place on wire racks to cool completely.

To make the glaze, combine the icing sugar, milk and vanilla extract in a bowl. Spoon over the rings and holes.

To decorate, top with the sprinkles or coat well in the icing sugar.

* dough

375 g (13 oz/2½ cups)
   plain (all-purpose) flour
2 teaspoons caster
   (superfine) sugar
150 g (5½ oz) cold
   unsalted butter,
   cut into 12 pieces
125 ml (4½ fl oz/½ cup)
   buttermilk

warm apple pie
bites

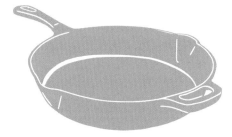

20 g (¾ oz) unsalted
  butter
400 g (14 oz/about 3)
  granny smith apples,
  peeled, cored
  and diced
45 g (1⅔ oz/¼ cup lightly
  packed) soft
  brown sugar
½ teaspoon ground
  cinnamon, plus
  2 teaspoons extra
  for coating
½ teaspoon ground
  nutmeg
2 tablespoons orange
  juice
2 teaspoons cornflour
2 teaspoons finely grated
  orange zest
220 g (7¾ oz/1 cup)
  caster (superfine) sugar
vegetable oil, for
  deep-frying

To make the dough, place the flour, sugar and butter in the bowl of a food processor and pulse until the mixture resembles breadcrumbs. Add the buttermilk and pulse until the dough comes together to form a ball. Turn out onto a floured surface, shape into a disc, wrap in plastic wrap and refrigerate for 2 hours.

Meanwhile, place the butter, apple, brown sugar, cinnamon and nutmeg in a frying pan over medium heat and cook for 5–6 minutes until the apple has softened. Combine the orange juice and cornflour to make a paste, add to the apple mixture and cook for 1 minute or until thickened. Add the orange zest and cool to room temperature.

Roll out the dough on a floured surface to 3 mm (⅛ inch) and, using a 9 cm (3½ inch) round cutter, cut out circles. Re-roll the scraps and repeat. Place 2 teaspoons of apple mixture in the centre of each circle, fold in half and pinch the edges together firmly to seal. Refrigerate for 15–20 minutes.

Combine the caster sugar and extra cinnamon together in a shallow bowl and set aside.

Heat the oil in a deep-fryer or large, heavy-based frying pan to 175°C (340°F). Deep-fry the pies, 3–4 at a time, for 1–2 minutes on each side until lightly golden. Drain on kitchen paper, then roll in the cinnamon sugar to coat. Serve immediately.

205

mini coconut
cakes

125 g (4½ oz) butter, at
   room temperature
165 g (5¾ oz/¾ cup)
   caster (superfine) sugar
1 egg
2 egg yolks
2 teaspoons natural
   coconut extract
125 ml (4½ fl oz/½ cup)
   coconut milk
185 g (6½ oz/1¼ cup) plain
   (all-purpose) flour
¼ teaspoon baking
   powder
¼ teaspoon bicarbonate
   of soda (baking soda)
35 g (1¼ oz/⅔ cup)
   coconut flakes

COCONUT FROSTING
2 egg whites
110 g (3¾ oz/½ cup) caster
   (superfine) sugar
3 tablespoons glucose
   syrup
icing flowers or 30 g
   (1 oz/½ cup) coconut
   flakes, toasted,
   for garnish

Preheat the oven to 180°C (350°F/Gas 4). Grease and flour a 12-hole 125 ml (4½ fl oz/½ cup) capacity friand tin.

Place the butter and sugar in the bowl of an electric mixer and beat on medium speed for 1–2 minutes until light and creamy. Add the egg and egg yolks one at a time, beating well after each addition. Mix in the coconut extract and coconut milk. Add the flour, baking powder and bicarbonate of soda and beat for 1 minute. Mix in the coconut flakes.

Divide the mixture between the friand moulds and bake for 20–25 minutes until golden and the cakes spring back lightly to the touch. Cool in the tin for 10 minutes, then turn out onto wire racks to cool completely.

To make the frosting, place the egg white, sugar, glucose and 2 tablespoons water in the top of a double boiler over medium heat and, using an electric beater, beat for 7 minutes or until stiff peaks form.

Immediately frost the cakes and garnish with icing flowers or coconut flakes.

mango lassi
rum pops

makes 18

550 ml (19 fl oz) mango
 pulp
120 ml (4 fl oz) white rum
120 ml (4 fl oz) orange
 juice
250 g (9 oz/1 cup)
 honey-flavoured
 yoghurt
4 tablespoons honey
½ teaspoon ground
 cardamom
1 teaspoon orange
 blossom water
18 popsicle sticks

Place all of the ingredients, except the popsicle sticks, in a large measuring jug and whisk to combine.

Pour into eighteen 60 ml (2 fl oz/¼ cup) capacity popsicle moulds. Cover with plastic wrap and insert a stick through the plastic into each pop. Freeze for 8–10 hours until completely frozen.

rocky road
pops

makes 30

80 g (2¾ oz) unsalted
  butter, at room
  temperature
125 g (4½ oz/1 cup) icing
  (confectioners') sugar
2 tablespoons cocoa
  powder
2 tablespoons pouring
  (single) cream
60 mini marshmallows
30 lollipop sticks
500 g (1 lb 2 oz) dark
  chocolate (65% cocoa
  solids), melted
125 g (4½ oz/1 cup) finely
  chopped walnuts

To make the chocolate cake, preheat the oven to 180°C
(350°F/Gas 4). Grease and line a 22 cm (8½ inch) round
cake tin with baking paper. Sift the flour and cocoa
together into a large bowl. Combine the sugar with 125 ml
(4½ fl oz/½ cup) boiling water in the top of a double boiler
over medium heat and stir until dissolved. Add the butter
and chocolate and stir until melted and smooth. Cool
slightly. Combine the egg and vanilla extract, add to the
flour mixture and mix well. Add the chocolate mixture and
mix well. Pour into the tin and bake for 30–35 minutes
until a skewer inserted comes out clean. Remove from
the tin and cool completely on a wire rack. Finely crumble
the cake into a large bowl.

Place the butter, icing sugar and cocoa in the bowl of
an electric mixer and beat for 1–2 minutes until light and
creamy. Add the cream and mix well. Add to the
crumbled cake and, using your hands, mix well; the
mixture should stick together when squeezed.

Line 2 baking trays with baking paper. Roll the mixture
into 30 g (1 oz) balls. Push 2 marshmallows into the centre
of each and roll to enclose. Insert a stick into each, place
on the trays and refrigerate for 30 minutes or until chilled
and firm.

Carefully dip each pop in the chocolate, gently twirling
off any excess. Roll each in the walnuts to coat well.
Stand upright in a piece of polystyrene to set. Serve
immediately or store in an airtight container in the
refrigerator for 3–4 days.

210

* chocolate cake

110 g (3¾ oz/¾ cup) self-
    raising (self-rising) flour
40 g (1½ oz/⅓ cup) cocoa
    powder
200 g (7 oz) caster
    (superfine) sugar
80 g (2¾ oz) unsalted
    butter, at room
    temperature
125 g (4½ oz) dark
    chocolate (65% cocoa
    solids), finely chopped
2 eggs, lightly beaten
1 teaspoon natural
    vanilla extract

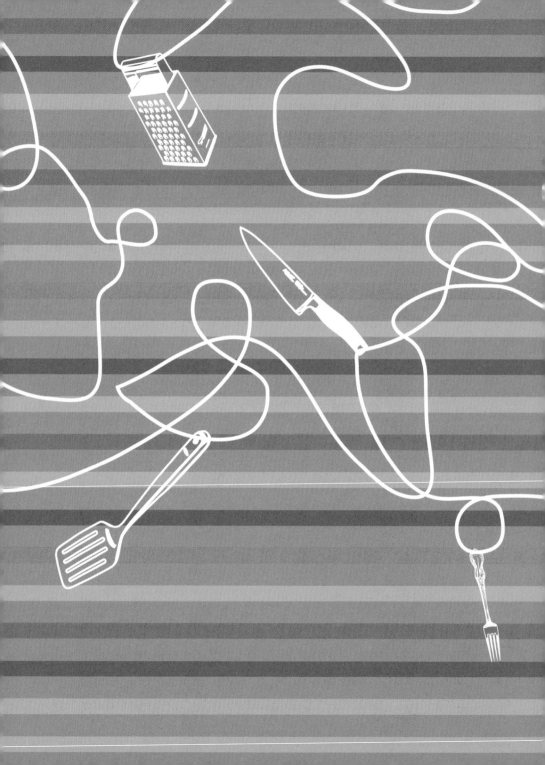

Index

A

almond corkscrews 189

apples
jelly appletinis 193
warm apple pie bites 205

B

banana daiquiri cupcakes 137
barramundi burgers with lemon
myrtle mayo 98

beans
cannellini bean and chorizo
empanadas 73
mini duck pies with broad
bean mash 90
pandan chicken and black
bean parcels 97

beef
beef and sherry pastries 102
parmesan wafers with celeriac
remoulade and roast beef 21
betel leaves with crab, kaffir
lime and chilli 57

berries
blueberry mojito popsicles 174
chocolate tarts with raspberry
185
lemon cheesecakes with
blueberry sauce 118
raspberry cupcakes with white
chocolate ganache 113
raspberry macarons with
white chocolate 114
strawberry tartlets with sticky
balsamic glaze 181
black cherry and kirsch jellies 190
black velvet whoopie pies 158
blood orange macarons 126
blueberry mojito popsicles 174
brownie bites with cheesecake
topping 146
brioche with orange, fennel and
grapes 33
brioche with scrambled eggs and
salmon caviar 18

C

caramel
dulche de leche cupcakes 117
peanut macarons with salted
caramel 166

pecan caramel tartlets 198
caramelised leek and artichoke
scones 105
caramelised onion baby tartes
tatin 37
cauliflower galettes with taleggio
and walnuts 106

cheese
cauliflower galettes with
taleggio and walnuts 106
chicken meatballs wrapped in
prosciutto 10
manchego croquettes with
sweet capsicum relish 69
parmesan wafers with celeriac
remoulade and roast beef 21
prosciutto, roquefort and
rocket arancini 53
smoked ham and cheddar
quichettes with green
tomato pickle 78
zucchini and haloumi fritters
with roasted capsicum
salsa 85
zucchini flower fritters stuffed
with feta and basil 46
see also goat's cheese

cheesecake
brownie bites with cheesecake
topping 146
lemon cheesecakes with
blueberry sauce 118
vanilla cheesecake pops with
ginger cookie crumbs 130

chicken
chicken meatballs wrapped in
prosciutto 10
chicken pizzettes with rosella
paste and macadamia
nuts 82
pandan chicken and black
bean parcels 97
preserved lemon, chicken and
radicchio quichettes 25
saffron chicken pies 94
tostadas with chipotle chicken
and guacamole 86

chickpeas
grilled eggplant and chickpea
fritters 14
spicy onion and chickpea
bhajis 45

chilli
churros with chilli-chocolate
sauce 194
crisp pork belly with chilli
caramel 65
pork tostadas with chilli
jam 66

chocolate
choc-mint whoopie pies with
marshmallow frosting 129
chocolate indulgence ice-
cream sandwiches 154
chocolate macarons with
espresso and cocoa nibs 145
chocolate tarts with raspberry
185
churros with chilli-chocolate
sauce 194
double chocolate whoopie
pies 162
hazelnut macarons with
chocolate and Frangelico 201
ice-cream cake pops 177
profiteroles with chocolate-
espresso sauce 122
raspberry cupcakes with white
chocolate ganache 113
raspberry macarons with
white chocolate 114
s'mores cupcakes 138
vanilla whoopie pies with
chocolate chips 186

chorizo
cannellini bean and chorizo
empanadas 73
prawn and chorizo pinchos
with paprika mayonnaise 13
churros with chilli-chocolate
sauce 194
coconut cakes, mini 206
crab cakes with wasabi avocado
70
crumpets with goat's curd and
lavender honey 97

cupcakes
banana daiquiri 137
dulche de leche 117
lemon meringue 141
raspberry, with white
chocolate ganache 113
s'mores cupcakes 138

D

duck
  mini duck pies with broad
    bean mash 90
  Peking duck and macadamia
    wontons 38
  Peking duck pancakes 26
dulche de leche cupcakes 117

E

eggs
  brioche with scrambled eggs
    and salmon caviar 18
  smoked trout, lime and quail
    egg tartlets 89

F

fig galettes with jamón and
  pepperberry mayo 101
fish and fennel pies with
  sourdough crust 62
florentines, Persian 178
fritters
  grilled eggplant and chickpea 14
  zucchini flower, stuffed with
    feta and basil 46
  zucchini and haloumi, with
    roasted capsicum salsa 85

G

g & t pops 150
ginger whoopie pies with spiced
  candied-ginger cream 133
gingersnap and peach ice-cream
  sandwiches 149
glitter pops 142
goat, Sri Lankan goat curry
  turnovers 93
goat's cheese
  brioche with orange, fennel
    and grapes 33
  crisp mushrooms stuffed with
    goat's cheese 34
  crumpets with goat's curd
    and lavender honey 97
  goat's cheese roulade on
    bruschetta 22
  pizzettes with goat's milk
    camembert and pickled
    walnut 77

grilled eggplant and chickpea
  fritters 14
gyoza with pork and kaffir
  lime 50

H

ham
  fig galettes with jamón and
    pepperberry mayo 101
  smoked ham and cheddar
    quichettes with green tomato
    pickle 78
hazelnut macarons with
  chocolate and Frangelico 201
hibiscus vodka pops 182

I

ice-cream cake pops 177
ice-cream sandwiches
  chocolate indulgence 154
  gingersnap and peach 149
  mint brownie 125

J

jellies
  black cherry and kirsch 190
  jelly appletinis 193
  layered, with citrus and
    pomegranate 121
  tangerine mimosa jellies 165

L

lamb filo rolls with cinnamon and
  currants 42
lemon
  lemon cheesecakes with
    blueberry sauce 118
  lemon madeleines with
    limoncello glaze 153
  lemon meringue cupcakes 141
  meyer lemon bars 169
lentil balls with lime and smoked
  paprika 29

M

macarons
  blood orange 126
  chocolate, with espresso and
    cocoa nibs 145
  hazelnut, with chocolate and
    Frangelico 201

passionfruit 173
peanut, with salted caramel 166
Persian rose 161
raspberry, with white
  chocolate 114
madeleines, lemon, with
  limoncello glaze 153
manchego croquettes with
  sweet capsicum relish 69
mango lassi rum pops 209
meatballs, chicken, wrapped in
  prosciutto 10
meyer lemon bars 169
mini coconut cakes 206
mint brownie ice-cream
  sandwiches 125
mushrooms
  crisp mushrooms stuffed with
    goat's cheese 34
  rabbit calzones with porcini
    and pine nuts 58
  wild mushroom tartlets 41

N

north African tuna and preserved
  lemon parcels 74

O

ocean trout tartare with potato
  rösti 30
onions
  caramelised onion baby tartes
    tatin 37
  spicy onion and chickpea
    bhajis 45

P

pandan chicken and black bean
  parcels 97
parmesan wafers with celeriac
  remoulade and roast beef 21
passionfruit macarons 173
peanut macarons with salted
  caramel 166
pecan caramel tartlets 198
Peking duck and macadamia
  wontons 38
Peking duck pancakes 26
Persian florentines 178
Persian rose macarons 161
Pimm's pops 157

215

pizzettes
chicken, with rosella paste and macadamia nuts 82
with goat's milk camembert and pickled walnut 77

pops
blueberry mojito popsicles 174
g & t pops 150
glitter pops 142
hibiscus vodka pops 182
ice-cream cake pops 177
mango lassi rum pops 209
Pimm's pops 157
rocky road pops 210
vanilla cheesecake pops with ginger cookie crumbs 130
walnut brownie pops 170
watermelon margarita pops with sweet and salty lime wedges 134

pork
crisp pork belly with chilli caramel 65
gyoza with pork and kaffir lime 50
pork tostadas with chilli jam 66
prawn and chorizo pinchos with paprika mayonnaise 13
prawn and ginger moneybags 49
preserved lemon, chicken and radicchio quichettes 25
profiteroles with chocolate-espresso sauce 122
prosciutto, roquefort and rocket arancini 53

Q
quichettes
preserved lemon, chicken and radicchio 25
smoked ham and cheddar, with green tomato pickle 78

R
rabbit calzones with porcini and pine nuts 58
raspberry cupcakes with white chocolate ganache 113

raspberry macarons with white chocolate 114
rocky road pops 210

S
s'mores cupcakes 138
saffron chicken pies 94
salmon and mango ceviche in endive boats 17
scallops, char-grilled, wrapped in prosciutto 81
scones, caramelised leek and artichoke 105

seafood
barramundi burgers with lemon myrtle mayo 98
betel leaves with crab, kaffir lime and chilli 57
brioche with scrambled eggs and salmon caviar 18
char-grilled scallops wrapped in prosciutto 81
crab cakes with wasabi avocado 70
fish and fennel pies with sourdough crust 62
north African tuna and preserved lemon parcels 74
ocean trout tartare with potato rösti 30
salmon and mango ceviche in endive boats 17
smoked trout, lime and quail egg tartlets 89
wasabi tuna with cucumber salad 61
smoked ham and cheddar, with green tomato pickle 78
spiced pumpkin whoopie pies with pecan mascarpone 197
spicy onion and chickpea bhajis 45
Sri Lankan goat curry turnovers 93
strawberry tartlets with sticky balsamic glaze 181

T
tangerine mimosa jellies 165
tartes tatin, caramelised onion baby 37
Thai corn fritters 54
tostadas with chipotle chicken and guacamole 86

V
vanilla cheesecake pops with ginger cookie crumbs 130
vanilla doughnuts and doughnut holes, glazed 202
vanilla whoopie pies with white chocolate chips 186

W
walnut brownie pops 170
warm apple pie bites 205
wasabi tuna with cucumber salad 61
watermelon margarita pops with sweet and salty lime wedges 134

whoopie pies
choc-mint, with marshmallow frosting 129
double chocolate 162
ginger, with spiced candied-ginger cream 133
black velvet 158
spiced pumpkin, with pecan mascarpone 197
vanilla, with white chocolate chips 186
wild mushroom tartlets 41

Z
zucchini flower fritters stuffed with feta and basil 46
zucchini and haloumi fritters with roasted capsicum salsa 85